Taking Action

Short Stories

by
John Clark Smith

First Edition: 2019
Rs. 200/-

Cyberwit.net
HIG 45 Kaushambi Kunj, Kalindipuram
Allahabad - 211011 (U.P.) India
http://www.cyberwit.net
Tel: +(91) 9415091004 +(91) (532) 2552257
E-mail: info@cyberwit.net

Printed at Repro India Limited.

To Susan

Preface

Most of the stories in this collection revolve around one theme: the need to change, to rebel, or to be courageous. Inevitably this means conflict with tradition, authority, or the status quo. The people in these stories do not sit still and wait for others to make the changes. They are, in different ways and degrees, activists, even if the change is so subtle only they may know it. The choices may be social, political, personal, spiritual or romantic. They can involve people of all ages, races, and religions. But the need to transform relationships, regimes, systems, traditions, and habits is common throughout. Of course, for each person who stands up for principles or who rebels against the old ways, there is a cost, sometimes a very steep cost.

The stories have a variety of approaches to this theme. There is a story about someone not betraying his mission even if it could mean his life; a woman who will not let her paralysis stop her from protesting; a man who must save his city by righteous behavior; another standing up for a person of a different faith, even under tragic circumstances; a woman who refuses to sacrifice her principles regardless of how much money she is offered; a man, one of the ninety-nine percent, taking to court one of the one percent who wants to put him out of business; another who changes because of his reflection about his neighbor's lawn; a young couple discovering their feelings in the harshest environment; a youth who finds how a simple act of affection can uplift him; the student who tires of watching her town's decline because of apathy; an older man and woman who find each other after renting in the same building for many years; a building that transforms how a wife sees herself and her husband; a man who awakens others by fierce questioning; and a woman who places all her hopes on India to help her find herself. There are also stories about those refusing to change or mature; several stories about how art and music have incredible effects; how a man goes to extremes to awaken awareness of environmental destruction; a fantasy about a sister who loves imperfection; how death enlightens two people; and a wife who year after year believes she can save her husband, mentally fractured by military service.

The flash fiction follows suit, though it might only be a glimpse, such as a child being given a secret she should not have, a man fearful of not leading a worthy life, the success of a church relative to basic bodily functions, an unappreciated father, the fate of prophets, a man watching his memories disappear before his eyes, and neighbors arguing about their car and lawns.

There are also a few exceptions. These are quick doors to a state of mind rather than a plot or description of character.

Thank you for sharing with me the journeys these stories tell.

John

Acknowledgements

Except for **Unwrapped**, the stories below were published under my pen name D. D. Renforth.

No Ship is Big Enough originally published by *c c & d Magazine* (June, 2016).

Quakes originally published by *The Storyteller Anthology* (March, 2016).

Dust on the Soul originally published by the *BellaOnline Literary Review* (Winter, 2017).

Mark and Amy in the Desert originally published by *Romance Magazine* (Vol. 4, No. 4, May 9, 2016).

Cave Man originally published by *The Ekphrastic Review* (May 28, 2016). The story also included a photo of the Ajanta Caves.

Looking in the Glass originally published in *The Ekphrastic Review* (October 23, 2017). It included color photos of Duchamp's *The Large Glass*, Raphael's *La Sposalizio* and recordings of Liszt's piano works "Sposalizio" and "Mephisto Waltz No. 1." These works and music are all available online for free.

Bella and the Billionaires originally published in the *c c & d Magazine* (August, 2017).

A Place to Murder Little Boys originally published by *Swept Magazine* (August 4, 2017).

Dandelions originally published by the *Taj Mahal Review* (June, 2019).

The Red Monk originally published by *The Ekphrastic Review* (January, 2017). This story was illustrated by a color photo of the Ellora Caves. Photos of Ellora are easily found online.

Donovan versus Donald originally published by *c c & d Magazine* (January, 2018).

A Hug originally published by *Edify Fiction Review* (Vol 1, Issue 3, June, 2017).

Quest for Fulfillment originally published in the *Indian Review* (February 13, 2017).

The Ice People originally published by *Swept Magazine* (June 3, 2016).

Locals Only originally published online by *c c & d Magazine* in February, 2019 and in print in September/October, 2019.

When You Shoot an Arrow originally published in the *Taj Mahal Review* (June, 2019).

Freckled Woman originally published by the *Woven Tale Press* (Summer, 2019).

Before Father Lost his Mind originally published by *Microfiction Monday Magazine* (November, 2016).

Bill Died and Left Me a Pig originally published by *Microfiction Monday Magazine* (December, 2016).

The Brand of A originally published by *The Ocotillo Review* (Vol 1, Summer, 2017).

Jerrold's Agreement originally published by *Swept Magazine* (October 13, 2016).

Screams originally published by *Page & Spine* (July 20, 2018).

The Art of Flying originally published by *Burningwood Literary Journal* (Vol. 87, July, 2018).

Dogs and Insects originally published by *The Enchanted File Cabinet (*Vol. 6, No. 24, June 2017).

Unwrapped originally published by *Edify Fiction* (Christmas in July edition, July, 2019).

Contents

No Ship is Big Enough

Kola sat up in a wheelchair in her small studio apartment, adjusted the confining belts with her right hand, looked down at the spoon with its large deep bowl, and could easily see her blond hair and long face reflected in an upside-down image. Her blue eyes and red lips were exaggerated. Her hair, tied back in a ponytail, seemed to glisten. Her nose had grown. Countless times she had performed this spoon ritual in many countries and cities, in the days when she was not crippled. She liked the spoon reflection. It made her look bigger than she was. Her image stared back at her, regardless where she was, what might happen, and what she was thinking. She was alive and big enough to take on the bad guys.

This particularly large spoon was a special gift from those who knew she liked spoons. It had a wide handle on which was engraved a woman on a raft with her arm up trying to halt a giant ship, though the carving only included the bow of the oil tanker. At the bottom in tiny words: "Nature thanks Kola Spanán."

Kola was that lady in the boat and she did stop that ship. Unfortunately, in her attempt to hold up a sign, her boat rocked, she fell backwardly on to a metal contraption she had brought along to hook herself to the ship, and severely and permanently injured her spinal cord.

She smiled at the spoon. Her teeth spread out before her in the bowl.

Beside the spoon was a group of items. Other than her head, her right arm, and her hand, she was paralyzed, so it was critical that everything was in easy reach. In front of the cereal bowl, spread neatly in a large semicircle on a wide tray, were a glass of orange juice, a tiny round clock, a harmonica, a small CD player with inbuilt speakers—her favorite CDs were in two large pockets on the side of her chair—a set of colored pencils upon a drawing pad, three books piled on top of one another, three rocks in a group, a phone, a small television, another small screen for satellite images, and a hand-held computer. Several wires flowed away in different directions.

'It's absurd,' she thought, 'absolutely absurd,' as she contorted her nose and mouth in various faces gazing into the spoon. 'Why would they want to talk to me about taxes?'

It was true, she had not paid any taxes for three years, but that was because she had made less than the minimum. She wasn't trying to hide anything. She had no secret source of money or ingenious way of disguising wealth so that she could cheat the government. She was one of the ninety-nine percent.

Perhaps it was a mistake. The government makes mistakes.

The thought of government mistakes immediately sent her mind on a familiar path of criticism and an equally constant habit of talking out loud to herself when she was frustrated or angry.

"They sure do make mistakes!" she mumbled to herself. "They made a mistake letting oil companies drill the waters. They made a mistake dumping toxic waste into the waters. They make a mistake letting beef companies level the rainforest. They made a mistake allowing coal and other companies to destroy the atmosphere. But those are huge mistakes. I am only one person. What mistakes have I made compared to those?"

She knew of several people the government had wrongly audited and a few they should have audited more carefully. The government audited the Augers who lived next door with their three kids and found nothing. They would have found something if they had audited their heart. The Augers, as they proudly admitted to anyone, contributed large cash donations to organizations that denied climate change.

"Waste! Yikes, audits are wrong," she concluded to Goldman her cat. "Unless the government is going to audit itself, right, Goldman?"

"Keep your eye on the ball, Mr. and Mrs. Government!" she shouted. "Look at the real problems! The need for renewable energy, pollution, unbelievable waste, poverty, infant mortality, the one percent, youth unemployment, millions with no health care and millions more who can't afford the health care they need, the twenty percent who finance the drug war, millions who can't afford an education, and so on, and so on. You have so much more important things to do than thrust your bureaucracy at me."

The phone rang. Kola reached over and touched a button on the phone, activating the speaker phone.

"Kola," she answered.

"It's Angie. Did you hear from Reg?"

"No," Kola said, "he has seven minutes more."

"Midge has not checked in," Angie said.

"Where are the media?" Kola asked.

"They're here."

Kola turned on the television and switched to channel four.

"The others?" Kola wondered.

"They're set" Angie replied.

Her computer beeped.

"OK," Kola said, "I have confirmation from Reg. Start right now."

Kola turned off the phone and watched the television screen with the sound off.

Ten minutes later, she turned on the sound.

"A few minutes ago," the reporter said, "four vice-presidents of Fortune five hundred corporations were abducted. They were on a boat tour and conference regarding their future investment in the area. All are from corporations involved in using the resources of the Amazon River and the rain forest. They were literally boxed, hooked, and taken into the jungle by helicopter by the mysterious activist group KOSPA, as you can see from this video supplied by them. This is the second time this year this group, which is more often involved in political and economic situations, has entered the environmental arena. The group has asked the companies to begin repairing the damage they have done to the rainforest and the disruption they have brought to the Amazon River cultures. They list ten travesties committed by these corporations. Here is the list."

The news channel then displayed the list for the viewer.

"The group has promised to release the executives. However, it has warned them and their companies that real abductions will occur if they do not halt the rape of the lungs of the planet. Government officials again say that they have no idea who KOSPA is or what KOSPA means. Nor do they know how the three were abducted. But they assume that compatriots of the group were on board the ship, so every person will be interrogated before they leave the ship."

Kola again turned down the sound of the television and looked at her satellite screen, then stared down at her spoon.

Goldman meowed nearby.

"Ha! Of course you don't know, you bureaucrats!" she said. "Do they, Goldman? And you know why? Because we're right in front of you! Ha!"

Goldman meowed again.

"How could you know us? You're looking for crazy people and none of us are crazy. You're crazy!"

A half an hour later, the phone rang again.

"Kola," she said.

"We got a problem," Reg said.

The sound of helicopter blades swirled loudly in the background.

"Good. It means we're causing trouble," Kola answered.

"God, I wish you were here," Reg said, "like the old days. I don't how to do this."

"I bet your face is all red, isn't it?"

"Yeah, it is," a female voice came on the phone too.

"Midge, you girl!" Kola said.

"Well, after all those lessons," Midge said, "yes, I can say I can pilot a helicopter, but we got a problem."

"Give the man a kiss for me," Kola said. "He did great!"

A big smacking sound could be heard.

"You know, don't you, that she didn't really kiss me," Reg said. "She could have, mind you, but she chose not to kiss me. I could use a kiss right about now, but no, no, she throws a fake one."

"What's the problem?" Kola asked.

"There are people on our patch!" Reg said.

"You're kidding of course," Kola said.

"No he's not. I screwed up," Midge said.

There was a moment pause.

"Put the bad boys back on the ship," Kola replied. "We made our point."

"What?" Reg said.

"Contact Angie on the boat, say we're bringing them back," Kola said. "You have time. It's only a couple of minutes away. The authorities won't be there for another fifteen minutes. Go!

"What about Sasha and Chang?" Midge asked. "They'll still on the patch and they're frightened. They think they're in cannibal country."

"Ah no," Kola said. "No, they're not. Tell them to dig a deep hole and bury themselves up to the neck. When the natives come near, tell them to crawl slowly out of the hole and start speaking loudly in a made-up language. I did it once. It works. The underworld is terrifying to all peoples. That will give them enough time for Midge and Reg to come back and pick them up."

In ten minutes, another television update appeared on Kola's screen:

"We have an update on the abduction. Here is a video of the executives being returned to the boat. No one expected them back this soon, but as you can see, they're on the deck and the helicopter has taken away the boxes and is out of sight. We assume that the government has made a deal. Oh, I've just learned we have the tour organizer, Ms. Angie Riddick. Hello Ms. Riddick. What can you tell us? How did this abduction occur?

"'Several activists were hidden on board. The helicopter came in, dropped the boxes, and the masked activists forced the executives, two men and one woman, by gunpoint into the boxes. The boxes and the activists were taken away by the helicopter. It happened so quickly. The return of the boxes also happened much more quickly than we assumed. The federal agents and police have not even arrived. It was over in a couple of hours. How brazen these people are!'"

Kola smiled at this remark of Angie and turned the television off.

"You're so naughty! I love it," Kola said. "Isn't she, Goldman?"

Kola pounded the right armrest in joy. "Yes! Yes! Yes!" Then she played the melody from the song, "I Will Survive" on her harmonica.

Kola still had not begun to eat. She would not eat while her team faced danger.

Another beep from the computer. She read the email. Midge, Reg, Sasha and Chang were on their way to the coast. Kola acknowledged the email, happy the cannibals did not show up, and requested that they call her around midnight.

As Barber's *Adagio* now sounded from her CD player Kola began to enjoy her breakfast and wondered where she had put all her tax receipts. **THE END**

Quakes

Emma and Tom stood on opposite sides of a small room with a double sink. Emma was a young brunette woman in shorts and a tank top. Tom was a young man with brown hair dressed in shorts and a sleeve-less t-shirt.

People were scurrying around, arranging or fixing the room, carrying clothes over their arms and shoulders, so furiously active that the temperature of the room increased.

Emma and Tom had been staring at each other for several minutes, each with a look of boredom and disappointment.

"I don't even know you," Emma said loudly to Tom as people crossed back and forth in front of them. "That was my sister! My sister, for god's sake."

"Yeah, your drunk sister, don't forget that!" Tom said. "What did I do? I kissed her on the neck, that's it!"

"She knew you were my boyfriend," Emma said.

"Talk to your sister. It's partly her fault too, right?"

Tom walked over to her. As he did, a woman came and handed them their clothes.

"How many times are they testing today?" Tom said to the woman.

The woman shrugged.

Emma put on a coral skirt that almost reached the floor, with a puffy sleeved flowery blouse that ended in a ruffled collar. They wound and piled up her long hair with a large pin and barrette. Tom put on jeans, a blue plaid shirt, a dark brown leather vest, a red kerchief around his neck and a Stetson on his head. His black boots had spurs. Around his hips he placed a holster with two pistols.

The red light flashed. Emma began scrubbing clothes in one sink, dipping them into the other sink, and hanging them up on a line that stretched from one wall to the other.

Tom stood looking out the window, his hips cocked and his hands on his holsters.

Suddenly the room began to move, the clothes line dropped, the floor cracked, and the two of them fell to the floor. The lanterns tumbled, and the room went dark.

"Oh, William, it's another quake," Emma said in a Western accent. "Where are you?"

"I'm right here, Louise, near the door," Tom replied with an even greater drawl. "Don't you worry. I'll protect you. Keep close to the wall."

"But the Ratkov gang! They've been waiting. The Sheriff will be busy. They'll ravage my sister. She's home alone."

"Don't you worry, little honey. I'll save her."

Tom stood up and opened the door.

"But you'll be killed," Emma said. "The quake has split the street and there's no way to get to my house."

"I'll be back, my darlin'. No quake is gonna stop me! You can trust me with your sister!'

Tom bent over to kiss Emma, but Emma turned away.

The lights and the room returned to normal.

"William is supposed to kiss Louise before he heads off into danger," Tom said, removing his costume items and handing them to an assistant.

"That's not going to happen even when I'm playing Louise," Emma stood up and removed her dress.

"You're going to hold this against me? Have you forgotten Al, your co-star in 'Freight Train'?"

"We were rehearsing," Emma said.

"Oh sure."

They walked toward and then into another room, this one with multi-colored neon lights and walls painted bright red, white, and gold. Both received another set of clothes. Emma put on over her shorts and tank top a cone-shaped dress that was made of blue florescent plastic, and a square headpiece of the same material that seemed to have a living snake moving in and out of it. The make-up artist pasted her face with glistening eye lids, caked pink cheeks, eyebrows of orange that curled, and bright and shining yellow lipstick. Her hair seemed to flow around the square hat like purple whipped cream.

Tom removed his clothes and was sprayed silver from head to toe, including his hair and face. He then put on a silver speedo bathing suit, pink inner tubes tight around his waist, chest, neck and head. He wore no shoes.

The room was empty except for a folded pile of clothes on a table and a slot in the wall that Emma could slide the clothes for washing and drying.

As they waited for the cue, Tom tried to put his arm around Emma but Emma wriggled away.

"You liked Al," Tom said.

"I did," Emma said. "So what!"

"I was jealous. Why did you get to kiss him? That other gal could have kissed him. It was always you kissing him, on the lips, many times. And I was watching."

"Oh my god, Tom, it was a romance! That was my role. You weren't acting with my sister."

The cue came and Emma picked up one of the pieces of clothing and began to feed the clothes into the slot while electronic avant-garde music played.

Then the room shook and the lights went off. They fell down together.

Emma spoke with a clipped almost robotic tone,

"Sis in hot fire, Cuddle Face."

Tom stood and walked in a jerky motion to the door.

"On it, warm bottom," Tom said. "Quake is baby-work for Cuddle Face!"

"Keep the plug, Cuddle Face," Emma said. The two squeaked.

The lights returned and the costume people reappeared and carefully removed Emma's costume and hosed down Tom to remove the silver paint.

As the assistants were working on them, the actors continued their conversation.

"Fine, I apologize," Tom said. "I shouldn't have put my arms around her and kissed her on the neck."

"And that's another thing," Emma said. "On the neck. Who does that when it's casual?"

Tom went over near her and stared straight at her.

"Will you marry me?" Tom asked, a broad smile following.

"No. You're an idiot. Marry my sister."

"Your sister's not my type. She's wants to cause trouble."

"What?" Emma said, perplexed by Tom's comment as they entered the next room, a laundromat in the basement of an apartment building.

Another round of costumes and make-up came. Both were splattered in fake blood, Emma had an arm hanging off her shoulder, with one eye not quite in its socket, with bruises all over her face. She wore a ripped nightgown with only a bra and panties underneath. Tom wore a police hat, a loose fitting full-length white gown, high heels, bags and dark circles under his eyes, and two fake large green neon tongue pins which he flashed as much as possible when he talked. He dragged a leg as he walked.

The room began to shake and the lights went off. A coffee cup fell off the laundry table.

Tom growled in a slow eerie gravelly bass voice:

"I'm going for your sister now. The quake won't stop me,"

"You promised you would leave her alone," Emma said in a high screechy terrified voice. "Please. Please leave us alone."

Emma dragged her body toward the door.

"Help! Help!" Emma screamed.

"Who's going to hear you? They're all in a panic. God I love a good quake. I want your sister so much. Tell me where she is or I'll take off the other arm and rip out the other eye and...."

"I can't," Emma said in tears. "I won't. You'll hurt her."

"Your sister hates you," Tom said. "Why do you care? HAHAHAHA! I'm going to make her my bride."

The lights snapped on and the room stops shaking.

Again the crew removed the costumes and makeup and Emma and Tom returned to their shorts and tops.

They went to a lunch room and began to eat quickly food set up in the middle of the room.

"What did you mean?" Emma said. "Why does she cause trouble?"

"Let's not get into it."

"What did she say?"

"It's not important."

"Tom! Stop it! I want to know."

"She was drunk, OK, and she came up and whispered in my ear, 'Kiss me on the neck and make Emma nervous.'"

"And you complied," Emma said.

"I thought it was a joke. I should have known. She knew you were watching. What a bitch! What's with the two of you?"

Emma sat quietly with her own thoughts for a minute.

"She's not your type?" Emma asked.

"I don't like manipulative and vindictive women who use men to get back at other women. That's what I think your sister is doing, I'm sorry to say. I'm not the only one who thinks that. She wants your life and wants to make you feel bad."

The room began to shake.

"What? What is that? What's going on?" Emma said. "We're off set, aren't we?"

Tom nodded.

The ceiling began to collapse in front of them.

"Quick, get under the table," Tom said. "It is Los Angeles, after all."

They huddled under the table and looked at each other, smiling. Then, as the items on the table fell over and made noises and the walls of the room began to crumble, they kissed.

"Yes, I'll marry you," Emma said.

A tree smashed through the front wall.

Emma added. "You think my sister's safe?"

THE END

Dust on the Soul

The death of Cecil's best friend was a mirror in which all of Cecil's life was a shadowy reflection. Losing his friend when so young was difficult to endure or understand and a clear indication to him that, if fate chose to take his friend, then many others should not pass the test of deserving life, including Cecil himself.

Before the death, Cecil had attended university, eventually earned a doctorate, and joined the faculty as the youngest ever staff member. After the death of his friend, Cecil saw his teaching job as a babysitter with spoiled and unappreciative students wasting their good fortune. Students soon revenged through their evaluations and Cecil resigned and returned to wallow in the same factory where he had had a summer job between university years as a line supervisor. There he could hide and freely let the despair triumph. There he could show his discontentment with the human race. There also he would set loose a darkness that had apparently been waiting within him. There he could grumble without consequences.

One of the few people Cecil exempted from his scorn and negativity was Julia, the sister of his deceased friend. Cecil, of course, had known Julia since childhood, had lived on the same street, and went to the same schools. At dances Cecil sat on one side of the gym and Julia sat on the other, neither participating in the fun. Both were shy, sullen, bookish, and unpopular, with few friends and no romances, while Julia's brother was a popular star athlete and the crush of many girls.

After her brother's death Julia jumped on a train to a profligate destination, the opposite life of the girl she seemed to be and the one Cecil knew in high school. Cecil ignored her behavior and never condemned or tried to correct her. Food and money he gave her without expecting them in return. He overlooked her loss of many jobs, her waste of money, her failure to pay her rent, and even a night in jail for misconduct. Even when she would appear at his door a few hours before daybreak, sometimes crying and heartbroken, or unaware of who or where she was, and sleep in his bed while he slept on the couch, he remained supportive.

"What's wrong with you?" Julia mocked him. "Why do you help me? Why are you always there? You don't even like me. When my brother was alive, you'd go out of your way to ignore me. And why are you always looking at me like that?"

Neither she nor anyone else had the answer to these questions. His fellow factory workers' explanation was that he was attracted to her. Why else would he be so kind to an obviously unappreciative woman? Continually he reminded them all that he did not like her romantically or even as a friend. A few wondered if he might be comforting her after the death of her brother, but that explanation he also denied strongly. Their common rage over the death had never been a bond between them. Nor could their past history and her present behavior and lifestyle offer reasons for why he disregarded his own darkness and treated her differently. Some other factor had encouraged him to stay near her, but to no one had he revealed that factor because it seemed so private and strange.

Then he had a casual encounter with a fellow factory employee, Paige, who worked both in the office and on the floor of the factory. Paige went to high school with Cecil and Julia. She had a thick red scar diagonally across her face and was very short, almost as short as a dwarf. Her small stature also made her stocky and overweight and this plus the scar were sources of ridicule by the guys in high school and on the factory floor, the men Cecil supervised.

Her appearance was unique, but it could not compare to her fiery personality, confidence and fearlessness. Paige was the office dragon, willing to snort oral fire at any sign of unfairness and always willing to defend herself or others. For that reason, no one, including the men in the factory, would ever attack her in person.

Paige knew about Cecil's moody and generally disgruntled personality, and Cecil knew about Paige's temperament, but they rarely had the opportunity to interact beyond the needs of their jobs. That changed one day when Cecil overheard the office clerks who reported to Paige talking about a popular television soap opera. Cecil in his usual grouchy attitude reacted by announcing that they were people without "taste."

"People with taste," he announced, "don't waste their time on such inferior writing, acting and plot lines. Find something better."

"Why don't you mind your own business?" Paige countered in support of her team.

"What's the matter? Don't want to hear the truth?" Cecil asked.

"Seriously," she continued, "go back to the floor. You make everyone nervous and depressed. Or shout at your walls at home. Leave us alone. You're just a bitter old man in a young man's body."

Because of the way his own team treated her, Cecil had sympathy for Paige and would have preferred to avoid sparring with her. Her attack quickly changed his mind.

"Really?" Cecil asked. "You think that show is for the intellectual giants of the world? The problem with you all is that you set your sights too low. You're all just looking for a husband so you can be baby machines and then have an excuse to watch one soap opera after another."

"Even if that was true, which it's not, at least we'd have a purpose," Paige said. "What happened to your purpose, Mr. Smarty Pants? I remember you in high school. So intelligent, so ambitious. Even taught at the university. Now look at you. Working at your summer job."

"Being only a baby machine is no better than being a lower animal," Cecil continued. "The universe gave you a brain. Use it."

"What do you know about me or any of us? At least we're not living the life of certain women you and I know. Or is destroying one's body and brain with drugs and alcohol and going from one measly job and man to another a sign of an intellectual giant? Why not go after her?!"

As he was about to counter-attack, he stopped himself and not only because he knew that Paige was correct. Julia was living a dissolute life and he had not tried to stop her. But he hesitated for the same reason he supported Julia, a reason that stretched back to the time of his friend's death, when the realization first had momentarily struck him. He had failed to clarify it to himself many times. He could only say that the experience seemed to lift him out from a morass or a cold place of shadows within him. Paige, like Julia, inexplicably had that magical capability. There was something in Paige's eyes that radiated a positive energy from being near her.

"Leave Julia out of this," he replied weakly.

"We're not all artists, poets and philosophers, you know," Paige said. "Consider our boss, what do you think he does to relax? He reads comic books and looks at porn. Go after him, why don't you? He's educated. He's got an engineering degree. Ha! But no, you're not going to attack him. Well, I'm not ashamed to admit it, I'm tired at night and I want to veg out. If I start to read a book—and I do read books and so does everyone else here—I go to sleep, that's how tired I am. I'm on my feet all day."

With that comment Paige turned and walked away. The office workers at their desk glared at him with emotionless faces, but inside they each shouted a victory, 'Yes! The dragon wins again! The monster is defeated!'

Cecil did feel defeated, but this defeat did not bother him because, even in the midst of the argument, Paige lit up something within him and reminded him of a time when he was a happier person.

At three o'clock the following morning, Cecil heard a heavy thump at the door that woke him up. He opened the front door and there laying across the doorstep was Julia crying and groaning. He stepped outside to see if she was with anyone, but he could only see a car speed off down the street in the darkness.

He picked her up, as he had done on other occasions, and laid her on his bed.

She opened her eyes and stared at him. A tear came down her cheek. Then she gagged and needed to regurgitate. He brought the pail and she threw up. Cecil wiped her lips with a wet cloth.

He noticed a stream of blood coming down her leg.

Julia could tell he was looking at the blood.

"They hurt me, Cecil," she said in between cries.

"Who? Who?" Cecil said.

"I don't know for sure. I wasn't fully conscious. They put something in my drink, I think."

Cecil called 911.

The ambulance came and took her to the hospital. The police eventually found the men who had assaulted her. They were among the men with whom she had often gone to clubs, took drugs, drank, and danced.

In the emergency cubicle at the hospital, as Cecil sat in a chair by her bed, Julia asked if he could stay with her for a while.

"I know you don't like me, Cecil," Julia said, "and I don't understand why you're always there for me. You never liked me, even when we were kids. You don't have to deny this. It's OK."

Cecil would not explain his reasons for watching out for her, not here, not in an emergency room.

"You want to be like my brother, don't you?" she said. "I know. My brother made you promise, didn't he?"

Cecil shook his head. Her brother never spoke to him about Julia.

"You really don't have to watch me anymore, Cecil. Not anymore. I'll be fine. I've had enough of this, more than enough. I'm a mess and I know it, and, you know what? I'm done. You did well. Considering you never liked me, I'd say you did very well."

She reached over and touched his hand.

"Thank you, Cecil, even if your kindness sometimes hurt me. I don't get it but thank you. If you had liked me and did what you did for me, then it would have been different, but I knew it wasn't that. Did you do it out of sympathy? Is that it?"

Again Cecil shook his head. His care for her had nothing to do with her brother or her brother's death. He had little sympathy for the way she treated herself.

"Fine. Deny it. Don't tell me," Julia said. "It doesn't matter."

Cecil avoided replying to her at that moment because he believed that whatever he said would hurt her feelings. He could never avoid the truth that he did not like her romantically or as a friend. He had no specific reason for why he did not like her; he was just not comfortable around her.

But something greater than chemistry drew him to her.

At work that week, Paige came up to Cecil and said, with her fists up in the air, as if she was ready to box.

"Do you want to fight some more? I've got time and lots to say."

"I bet you do," Cecil said. "But no. Maybe later,"

"We heard about Julia. I'm sorry, Cecil. We all wish her well. We really do."

"Thanks," Cecil said. "She's just got out of the hospital and is determined to start a new life. Of course, her partying friends call because they want her to return to the old ways but she doesn't want to. The few friends she had from high school had long ago dropped her. So she's really lonely and stuck with me. I'll tell her what you said. She'd appreciate you asking about her."

Cecil was about to walk away, but she stopped him.

"And there's something else. We all heard what you said about me to the guys on the floor," Paige said.

"I spoke the truth," Cecil said. "You'd be the best union representative for them. No one can fight for others' rights better than you, I'm sure of it."

"Well, guess what? They voted me in," Paige said, doing a little dance before him.

"Great. So they should. Everyone has a giant inside, but few can show it to others. You're one of those who can."

"I don't understand," Paige said. "Those guys would never have supported me without you. They sometimes even make fun of me. But you stood up for me. Why? You're not even in the union. And you're such a monster usually."

Cecil smiled.

"Let's just say, I'm in and out of darkness."

"But why support me?"

There were two reasons, but Cecil decided not to share them both. The key reason he recommended her was that she deserved it. None of the other candidates was as articulate or as passionate as Paige. But the other reason was that she reminded him of something that happened to him on the day Julia's brother died. As he was thinking about how unfair was his friend's death, he sensed in that moment that he was outside the sorrow and harshness of life, the darkness, and saw who he was and the beauty in others, in nature, and reality. A light rushed upon his soul. And from it he was so alive and so unbelievably relieved and uplifted. Everything seemed to make sense. But soon that glimpse was over and something like a giant stone was rolled across the entrance to his life again and shut off that vision and he slid back into a darkness, where everything was selfish and false. He wasn't sure how or why he had the experience, but it happened and for a brief period he had a flash, a feeling, of how extraordinary life was. Afterwards, he suppressed the experience, thinking it was crazy, but he could not forget it.

He tried so hard to recapture that moment of light. He tried at the university, at work, and through meditation. Nothing worked until he saw Julia by accident one afternoon at her brother's gravesite. She was recovering from another wild night, she had been crying, but he looked into her eyes and could see that light again and for a couple of seconds the darkness vanished. The light was dim and the feeling shallow, but it was present. So he hung on to it, hung on to her, because she gave him the hope of light. Now he looked for it in everyone and had found it in a few others, but most people affirmed the dark and the selfish and the vicious and were sticking needles in him; after a time, these needles injected a disease and began to affect him so much he could not control it. He had a harder and harder time seeing that light in others, though it occasionally did happen. Anger and depression followed.

Then the other day, when he was quarrelling with Paige, the light burst from Paige. It was a much more powerful light than the light from Julia or at his friend's funeral, and once again he was so happy. It broke up for a couple of seconds the black cloud of ignorance and selfishness that had blocked him. The darkness had covered him like dust on the clear mirror of his soul and the dust has become so thick that no light from others could be reflected in it and he could not even see himself. But occasionally there was Julia and others, and now Paige. She was an inspiration, a flame that reignited the barely burning embers of his soul.

Cecil laughed.

"Why? Because none of those guys can compare to you as a rep and they know it. You're going to be a great union representative. Keep that spirit of yours. It's great."

"Thank you," Paige said, blushing, almost embarrassed by his speech. "I don't know what to say. I'll try my best."

She walked away, but, after sitting at to her desk for several minutes, she went back to his office. Cecil was working on his computer and did not see her standing at the door. She was unsure whether to speak her mind in this situation, but his comments encouraged her.

"I was thinking," she said to Cecil, "could I have Julia's cell phone number? There's a couple of things I want to talk to her about. For one thing, we could use another person on my team. I'm going to meet her for coffee. And Cecil, thank you again, you've brought a bit of light into my life."

THE END

Mark and Amy in the Desert

"Mark! Get up!" Amy said, standing over her friend in the desert heat. "We must be close."

Only someone who had weathered the desert and knew the signs could have such hope. To anyone else, the truth would seem bleak. There was nothing in sight but bare mountains, sand, lizards, rocks, cacti, tumbleweeds, and their own rapidly disappearing footprints. Mostly it was sun and the brutal glare of sun. Somewhere, in one direction or another, there was a road. Somewhere there was an oasis. But to the untrained eye, the expanse seemed to be endless nothingness with not a trace of mystery.

"C'mon, get up," Amy repeated. "You can do it! We have to keep moving. You and I are going to make it!"

Mark did not move. He was alive, but he sensed no life in him. His eyeballs were dry. His lips were split and parched. Though he had a wide hat covering his shaved head, he believed that he was cooking something on it. He wanted water, rest, and real food.

Amy brought out a catalogue.

"Here! Look at her! Isn't she pretty?"

Amy was showing him a photo from a match making catalogue that included photos of potential male and female mates in skimpy bathing suits, their measurements, personalities and interests. Most of them were from Russia, Eastern Europe and small Asian nations, young adults anxious to start new lives in better circumstances, the equivalent of mail order brides or grooms.

Choosing any mate from the catalogue was one of the incentives in a survival contest Amy and Mark had entered. The other incentive was one million dollars. They paid fifty thousand dollars each to endure the harsh conditions of the desert and complete the maze in a certain number of days. They needed only to finish the game together and each of them could select a mate from the catalogue and take the money. If they did not like the mates, they still had the million.

The idea came from a match-making company, Spouses Inc., who wanted to combine their service with the idea of a popular survival television program.

The tests were mazes and treasure hunts through difficult environments in fourteen days. The rules said that they could not travel at night, making the desert maze even more strenuous. Each maze had three escape routes and survival items, such as water, food and other useful items, were hidden along the routes.

"I don't care about the women. I don't think I ever did," Mark said, starting to slur his words after ten days of the grueling trek through the desert. He had only four days left to complete the task, but these four days, they knew, would be the worst.

"You don't mean that," Amy said, trying to lift Mark to his feet, and shoving the catalogue before his eyes. "That's why you wanted to do this, remember? You've such a hard time meeting someone. Look at her! Her name is Vanessa. Think about you and Vanessa together and…Wow! Look at the breasts on Regina, Mark!"

The breast comment was Amy's way of starting a conversation and making him more alert. She knew Mark had a selective eye when it concerned breasts.

"Sand! That's all I can think about. I have sand on every inch of my body, in every opening. All the holes of my body! When I walk, and my skin meets other skin, it's like sandpaper rubbing sand paper. My ass is a sandpit. And yet you, you have the water."

"So you brought me to the desert to kill me?" Amy asked.

"Yep!" Mark jumped on Amy and began to choke her.

It was a game they played. One would say, 'So you brought me here to kill me,' and the other would try to choke the other.

Mark rolled off Amy and Amy laughed.

Amy had resisted catering to Mark's growing negativity, but she acquiesced now and brought out a water bottle. She hoped it would last for a few more hours, because she could never know when or where there were other hidden stashes of water bottles on route.

Mark ripped it from Amy's hand and began to devour it. He would have finished the bottle, but Amy took it back and put it in her bag.

"What about the money?" Amy said. "One million if we just get through this. What about your dream project?"

"I don't care! I could drink a jug of water and I'd still be burning up. I want to be home with a good book, listening to Bach, and looking forward to the upcoming Mondrian showing at the art gallery. You can have the money."

"We both have to finish," Amy reminded him. "No rewards for just one."

Mark stood up and then collapsed face down to the sand. He was exhausted as well as hot. The sun burned up every molecule of water in the air, making it difficult to breathe.

"You should have chosen someone else for this," Mark said when he sat up. "I'm not in as good as shape as you. But then I'm not a survivalist. Why me?"

Amy often wanted to quit too, but they were too close to the end to quit. They only had to find some path and they would have success.

"I didn't choose you. You asked me!" Amy said.

"Ok, fine. You're right. I did ask you. You being here makes sense. You're in great shape and you're a better companion for the desert. Well, that, and you have this perfect body."

"I do?" Amy said coyly, posing herself and walking around like a model, with an intentionally big smile with teeth. "You think I have a perfect body?"

Her smile woke him up. His sand covered face looked at her sand covered face—and now wide smile—and offered his own smile behind the covering.

Mark raised his eyebrows and looked her up and down and nodded several times.

"Oh yeah!" Mark said. "And I should know!"

"Stop it, you idiot," she said, laughing and punching him in the arm.

Mark did know her body well. They had seen each other's nude bodies often since they were six. Both of their parents were members of a nudist group and were regulars with their children at the local nudist club, nudist resorts, and beaches.

Her toned form was no accident. Amy not only used often a membership at a gym, but she would constantly sign up for challenging outdoor adventures. She would never call her body 'perfect,' but the exercise combined with skin care, good nutrition, and Kung Fu certainly might make some people think so. From Mark, nonetheless, it was a compliment. Mark had seen hundreds of nude bodies throughout the world when his parents traveled and visited nudist resorts and beaches.

Amy would like to return the compliment, but if she did, he would know she would be lying, especially before he trained for this contest. Before the training, he was tall and lithe, long limbs, with undeveloped muscles everywhere, a boy's body, except for his broad shoulders and a chest with some semblance of muscles and shape. His athletic parents were the only explanation for the chest. The almost hairless chest and back in his case emphasized the effeminate quality of his physique. A lack of muscles and strength was the result of his lack of interest in sports, exercise, and activity.

This attitude about exercising was irksome to Amy. Amy tried for years to coerce him into hiking, biking, camping, tennis, climbing, and so on, and he would sometimes oblige, he said, "because I love you." His true comforts were books, classical music, and art. The only reason he would occasionally accompany her on her adventures was because she would go on his activities, to his concerts, operas and galleries. He needed her company, he claimed, because he had no one else. When he found someone attractive, she would not like his hobbies. The truth is he never made much effort to find dates and relied on Amy.

Imagine her surprise when he asked her to join him in this extreme contest. She knew he was frustrated with his lack of success finding the right gal, so she could see how the catalogue of sexy women might excite him. The need for money was also a motivation. Mark was a teacher with a small salary. His dream was to start up an organization "to change the world," so the million dollars was very tempting. The big enigma to Amy was Mark thinking he could win the woman and the money through arduous physical activity and endurance. When he came up with the idea, Amy initially said no because the catalogue aspect bothered her. She could not see her own future with some unknown guy out of a catalogue, even though the men were often quite attractive. The challenge of the desert interested her but it was not so different from escapades she had already done without Mark. She had nothing to prove. The money was not as important to her as it was to Mark, though she did not want to lose her fifty thousand. The deciding factor for her was the thought of Mark with some woman who may not watch out for him in the desert. Amy on several escapades had seen many much fitter people than Mark have accidents or breakdowns. Her best friend Mark was not going to be one of them.

She finally agreed as long as Mark would train with her. They entered their names and waited to see if they would be the couple chosen. After several months of training, they both passed the physicals and waited for the day. Mark's body had dramatically changed from the training, but Mark was Mark, and, with no surprise to Amy, on day ten in the desert the old Mark appeared in full color. She also knew that his new body would disappear once Mark was home and returned to his old habits. This body was simply a front with no future.

The conditions were indeed extreme in every scenario, but the desert maze, with its highest prize of a million dollars, was the most grueling. No couple had yet completed it. The main obstacle was not lack of food, water, or protection, but the desert's effect on the mind. Each of the couples before them had at least one member who became delirious or started to see mirages and illusions. One had attacked the other during a delusion. Yet no one was seriously hurt because no one was ever in danger of losing anything but money and pride. Help was always available. Someone constantly, even while they were sleeping, was monitoring their vitals from the ground. A satellite was filming each step and both had microphones on them. In this sense, the situation was never life-threatening. If Mark's health was compromised, the medical team would have removed him. Had Amy known how safe the test was, she may not have entered it.

By the tenth day Mark had reached the stage mentally of the prior desert contestants. He no longer cared about the prizes. He did not have Amy's mental experience and physical stamina. He wanted to convince Amy to quit and go home. His body and spirit were famished and his mind more often than not now saw this whole idea as stupid, a costly but powerful lesson. He must give up his dream, he thought, be realistic, and accept his single status. After all, he had Amy.

Because of her experience and confidence, Amy could be more practical. She had thought of ways to keep Mark focused on the goal and at the same time distract him from both the discomfort he was experiencing and the mindless expanse they faced each day. Now she had reached an impasse. No ideas came to her except the old ones—make him angry or make him happy—but she had little faith in either of these options. Her attempts to create conflicts in the end failed. They did have arguments, but they never lasted. If she was mean and hurtful, she might lose her best friend. Making him angry, she quickly concluded, would not work.

Make him happy? Up to now only two things about going to the desert seemed to excite him: getting money for his dream project and finding someone who loved him. She had reminded him often about the money and the woman he would win if he completed the contest. That tactic had worked up till today. Now neither of them seemed to be driving him. On the contrary, he laughed about getting a woman out of this drudgery.

"I thought you wanted someone to love you," Amy said while she was using the binoculars the sponsors gave them to find signs of treasure or 'maze walls.'

Maze walls were sand colored posts that helped define the direction of the maze but were difficult to see except at a distance. The only clue was that they made a slight shadow, which in the binoculars was a dark line.

"Look at these women!" Amy said, pulling out the magazine again. "They're gorgeous. This woman could be the one,"

"Are you serious?" Mark scoffed. "You really think I'm going to find true love in a catalogue? That doesn't sound like you. How desperate do you think I am? I don't even believe in true love. I just thought, I thought, you know, I don't know what I thought, to be honest. I've tried everything else, and these women were so hot, I mean, who knows, it's worked for others. Forget it! It's stupid. The money was well-spent to teach me a lesson. So let's resign. I'll find a way to pay your share. I can't take another four days of this. I think I'm getting sick. The desert reminds me how barren is my heart."

"That's poetic, but we're not done," Amy said. "Your heart isn't barren. And you're not sick. Not really sick. If you were, they'd be rushing in here.

"OK, maybe I'm not dying, but I feel a pain here in my chest and I want to throw up, and I'm starting to see things, especially about myself, and I don't like it."

"Go ahead, throw up," Amy said. "You've got a whole desert. Just don't whine. You and I can make it."

Amy raced off ahead. She saw something. It looked like a treasure.

"OK, you're not being nice," Mark yelled after her. "Right now, I need a girlfriend, not a best friend."

That was it, Amy thought as she ran. He needs a girlfriend.

The treasure was a large umbrella to shade them from the sun. They had found a smaller umbrella in a previous treasure, but this one was so much better. It was big enough to shade them both. With every treasure, there was also a big bottle of water and some energy bars.

But how does she at this point convince her best friend to see her as a girlfriend? They knew each other so well. They could fart in front of each other, talk about each other's embarrassing habits, share intimate details of their fantasies, and recount stories of their dates. Amy spoke first with Mark when she wondered if she had a lump on her breast. Nothing was concealed. Mark knew every single mood and personality trait of Amy. He knew her opinions and quirks. The most mundane matters, such as her least favorite foods and when she liked to defecate, were as familiar to him as his own habits. When she became sick with a severe flu while her parents were on holiday in Europe, she asked for him, not any of her girlfriends. For a week Mark fed her, washed her, changed her bedding and clothes, slept near her, and listened to her delirium. Not once did he complain or expect her to choose anyone else.

Of course, they knew each other bodies well from nudist communities. They had never had sex and they had only kissed once on the lips, when they were twelve. The kiss was not memorable. Once, after a night of drinking, something could have happened when in the morning they found themselves together naked with their arms around each other, facing each other, on the beach. Amy's nudist parents dragged their children from the beach and threw the two of them, both unconscious, into the bed together. They remained stoned in that position throughout the night. The parents had a chore awakening them, still in a stupor from the previous night. Nothing transpired. Besides it was not the first time they had slept in the same bed or on the beach nude without intimacy. They had also used each other as dates or chaperoned each other to dances and other functions. Being with each other was never uncomfortable and on a few occasions people wondered why they were not a couple, to which they both said the same thing, 'there's no mystery.'

'No mystery. Can I become mysterious?' Amy wondered. 'I doubt it. Four days is plenty of time to go from stranger to girlfriend, but from friend to girlfriend is a more difficult leap. The more we know someone, the less likely the person will fall into the traps of seduction.'

In Amy's case, the task seemed insurmountable. There was no mystery, only the truth of their many years of friendship. In any case, the dilemma inspired an idea. This situation seemed the ideal time to ask a question that had nagged her the last couple of years. Maybe the question itself might keep Mark alert.

Mark was resting now in the cool shade under the umbrella. He seemed to have calmed down a little. Amy joined him.

"Don't resign just yet," Amy said.

"Why? Look, I'm sorry. Sure, physically I may, may make it, but I don't have your mental fortitude. I see everything in a different way. The desert is a curse. Sometimes I want to sabotage the whole thing by slicing myself. What's going on in my head is shameful. I'm having those delusions the company warned us about. I know you'll lose your money, but I'll pay you back. Four more days! Are you kidding? That's brutal."

"I want to talk with you."

"What is it?"

"You and I are thirty years old," Amy started.

"OK. Yes. Where's this going? We're the same age. Old folk."

"I was thinking…" Amy started to say.

"…why we're here in the desert under an umbrella?" he finished her thought.

"No. Well, yes. We're both still unmarried," Amy said bluntly. "Don't you wonder…?

"My god, Amy, don't you worry, you'll find someone, you're beautiful, you're smart, you're kind, you have a perfect body.'

'Stop it with the body!" she said.

"But…you just have high standards," Mark said.

Amy took a drink of water, offered it to Mark who surprisingly did not take it.

"Maybe we should be in that catalogue," Amy said. "Maybe we're on the wrong end.'

Mark looked up under his hood and stared at her.

"Seriously?" He asked.

She nodded.

"I'm afraid, Mark," Amy said, "really afraid. Aren't you afraid?"

"Afraid of what?" he asked, turning toward her.

"I'm never going to find the right person. Never. I've dated all kinds of guys, but nothing works out. Most of my friends seemed to be with the wrong people. They're always complaining. I don't want that, but I don't want to die alone. Do you ever feel that way?"

Like a big white cloud floating in the burning sun, a kindly pause hung there for some time, unwilling to move, but ready to give shade, allowing time for reflection.

She knew Mark was in the same situation. He had dated much less and had had far fewer people interested in him.

Mark had thought about being alone but on every occasion the face of Amy filled his mind. As long as Amy was around somewhere, he'd be fine, he thought.

"And I think, I think, you're the reason I'm alone," Amy finally confessed.

Another pause intervened, a long enough pause for Mark to consider his own life.

"Well that's not good," Mark said. "Because you're the reason for me too. Even in this situation, I thought, 'who cares about the fifty thousand, I have Amy.'"

"It's not good," Amy said. "Not good at all."

"In fact, it's very bad," Mark agreed.

A slight but lasting wind swept over the land, bringing up the sand. Mark held the umbrella in the direction of the wind. Both huddled close to each other as the sand whizzed by them.

Suddenly they both stood up and stared at each other. Together they shouted:

"So! You brought me to the desert to kill me."

"Yep!" They both answered.

Amy pushed Mark to the ground and jumped on him. They began to choke each other at the same time.

This time, when Amy stopped choking her old friend of twenty-four years and still straddling him, they stared at each other for a while, their faces a few inches from each other—though their faces were almost completely covered by sand and a sun protector—and smiled. They stared into each other's eyes and saw thousands of moments together. Both wondered who they would be without the other. It was a moment of revelation and recognition for them.

The cloud moved over them and the wind stopped for a moment.

Amy, who had studied the desert for several months before this challenge, turned her eyes briefly to the scene around them. Now she saw this harsh environment as magic. Each life form here had to work hard to remain, and many of those that survived were gloriously unique. What plant, she thought, was like the cactus which not even the vicious burning of the sun can faze? What plant seeded itself like the tumbleweed? What animal was like the camel or the desert jack rabbit whose giant ears release heat? To the untrained eye, the desert seemed an endless surface of death and emptiness, but sameness was deceptive. Under its surface were numerous creatures waiting for the cool of the night. The blistering noonday sun yielded, they had seen each day, beautiful skies at dawn and dusk, and only the rain forest had a greater variety of life forms. What seemed boring was mysterious and what was mysterious was the result of adaptation.

She brought her eyes back to Mark and somehow he and she, laden with sand, were one. To someone in the distance, they would have merged with the desert; no binoculars could find them. The feeling drew her closer than ever to him. She wanted to say something that expressed how she felt, but there were no words, just a feeling of bonding.

Amy started to climb off him, when Mark said,

"Where you going?"

Amy turned back and just as her face met his again, he held her head gently and gave a long sandy kiss. It was their second kiss, but this one was much more memorable.

*

They finished the contest but did not choose mates from the catalogue. In that choice the mystery had come to light.

We might ask, if we believed in such things, whether the desert had lured them there to join its strange array of creatures who have learned how to survive in the sun's scorching heat of relationships.

THE END

Cave Man

India 1853. As Buddhist monks chanted very quietly outside, a bearded, disheveled, dirty, with a paint splattered face and clothes, Preston Morrison slept on a carved nook in the rear wall of a cave, a blanket covering him. There was a large sketchbook beside him, on the wall hung his army uniform, and leaning up against the wall was a gun. The entrance to the cave was directly opposite to him, and beyond the entrance a cliff. It was daylight, but Preston had worked all night at his copying and forgot to snuff out the small fires across the front of the cave entrance to scare off wild animals.

The light from the fires revealed that all the walls of the cave were painted, though they were too dark and distant for anyone but Preston to see them clearly without a lantern. In the center of the cave was a massive sculpture of Buddha, whose head almost reached the cave ceiling, and around which there was barely enough room to walk.

*

The present. The tour guide entered the cave, stepped around the fires, stopped and spoke to the tourists in a styled, arrogant, insincere and professional voice,

"Now please stop here and huddle together so that you can see this fresco behind me. Watch out for the fires that either the natives use to frighten off tigers when they're working or the monks when they're sleeping.

"This particular work, only partially restored for reasons I'll explain presently, was painted by local artists and wandering Buddhist priests while taking respite from the monsoon and inclement weather. No one knows the names of these artists, but we do know that many of them were ascetics who lived off the local

villagers and traveling tradespeople. To these and other caves they would come for meditation and community with other monks.

"You will note that most of the symbols of the work have been damaged or obliterated. Various religious zealots from different sects attacked the work and sliced sections off the wall. What remains is a bodhisattva—a being that foregoes nirvana in order to save others—garbed in the fashions of the princes of those days, holding a lotus flower. Note how well the artist has captured the real-life posture and expression of the body, and how transcendent is the look on the bodhisattva's face."

"Please follow me quickly," the tour guide said, *"and we will examine a different kind of Buddhist cave next door."*

*

Preston was having a nightmare, one of many. For a minute he moved around restlessly in his bed, groaning and talking incoherently, then he jumped out suddenly, grabbed the gun, pointed it forward, walked around the statue as if searching for something, mumbling to himself without sense. His eyes were very large and scared. He then returned to his bed and laid down. A minute later he was startled by what he thought were the growls of a tiger beyond the entrance to the cave. He anxiously grabbed a thick stick, ignited the end of it, and walked to the entrance waving the lit end. The tiger, he thought, snarled and continued to growl. Preston walked back and forth across the entrance waving the stick at the tiger. He leaned down and threw a few sticks on one of the fires that seemed to be going out, yawned, returned to his bed, and lay down exhausted.

Then the tiger growled again, much louder, and only stopped after Preston sat up, shook his head, then picked up his sketchbook and the burning stick, walked over to a section of the cave, shoved the stick in the wall for light, opened up his sketchbook to a particular page, yawned, and began to copy the paintings sitting in the same lotus position as the statue. He painted for a while, then his head dropped, and he fell asleep.

The fires went out and the cave became dark for a brief period, then a dim light returned.

*

The tour guide returned with another smaller group of people and stood in front of the Buddha. The tourists stood to the right of the Buddha.

"Please watch your step," the tour guide said. "Sir! Please do not wander off. Thank you. The lights as you can see are very dim in this cave because the paintings on the walls are very sensitive and are slowly deteriorating even without light. You've been told not to take any flash photographs and I would hope that you'll abide by the rules. These caves were usually either living quarters or places for religious ceremony and meditation and were carved out of solid rock. Around the edges you'd see paintings of the various reincarnated lives of Buddha, known as The Jataka Tales. In the center of the room would be an enormous statue and/or a bell-shaped structure. Let's walk around it and then exit."

They slowly walk around the sculpture of Buddha as the tour guide continued.

"This path we are taking is the exact path that the Buddhist would take in meditation. People didn't live in this sort of cave. You won't notice any of the little stone ledges or rock-cut compartments that we've seen in other caves. This cave was only for meditation and ceremony. Imagine if you can what it must have been like for these people of old, in a time when there were still many Buddhists in India, and how these monks chipped away at this cave rock to hollow out these caves for revelation. Imagine also how they expected no recognition and yet they created these wonderful works of art. My assistant will now briefly flash some light on each of the paintings around the hall. Please do not touch them or come too near them."

A spotlight moved across several paintings as the tour guide and tourists left the cave.

*

Preston was in the lotus position with his head hung, the sketchbook on his lap. However, at every wall and at the sculpture there stood monks in long orange hooded robes painting. Sculpting, and repairing.

The monks disappeared when Parvati, a young local woman, Sanchi, her father, Commander White and Lieutenant Fisk, two British army officers, entered, all out of breath after climbing the cliff to reach the cave. White and Fisk violently swatted at bees as they entered. Parvati carried a sack and Fisk two large bags.

They saw Preston asleep. White, Fisk and Sanchi walked around and looked at the frescoes while Parvati shook Preston gently.

Preston awoke and saw Parvati.

"Parvati!" he said joyfully.

Preston reached out to hug her, but she shyly pointed to the others with her.

"What bliss! To see your face first as I open my eyes."

Parvati took his hand and brought Preston to Sanchi, Fisk and White, and they greeted each other.

"And my friend returns," Preston said to Fisk, "looking weary from the journey, even dragging up the mountain the Commander. Welcome!"

Preston shook heartily the hands of Fisk and White.

Preston extended his hand to Sanchi.

"And you, father of Parvati, will always find a friend in me. Thank you for coming. You may now see how brilliantly your daughter has copied some of these works. But I sense in you all bring some sad message."

Sanchi shook Preston's hand.

Parvati excitedly ran over, picked up the sketchbook, returned, and showed proudly Preston's work to Sanchi, White, and Fisk. They all examined the book.

Preston went to a corner of the cave, returned with a bag of coins and offered them to Sanchi.

Sanchi took the bag and looked inside it.

"A small reward for your people helping to unearth this artistic miracle," Preston said.

"I thank you for your gift," Sanchi said with a heavy accent but clearly. "And I thank you for your most kind affection and admiration for Parvati. Still I must speak to you openly. I and others from the village have become fearful of this place. Many think we should have left the caves untouched. Our villagers have had many misfortunes since we cleared the caves out with you. The tigers have multiplied. None of the villagers want to continue the work, and I urge you too to abandon this place. We fear for you. Here the tigers now rule. Here many men have died. What does this mean? It means that Allah does not want us here. Indra has cursed us all. I hope and pray that you will leave for your safety.

"I have also forbidden my daughter from returning, since there'll be no one to accompany her. If you want to see her, you must come to the village. And I believe that the people of the village will not accept her if she comes here anymore. They will call her sorceress."

Sanchi waved his arms around the walls.

"All this is against the prophet and should remain in darkness."

"Sanchi," Preston pleaded, "we have trod this path before. There is nothing to fear..."

Sanchi shook his head, waved his hand to interrupt him, extended his hand to Preston, shook it again and quickly exited, beckoning also Parvati.

Parvati and Preston approached each other closely and looked into each other's eyes for a moment, then she departed with Sanchi.

"Parvati," Preston said tenderly and quietly.

He followed after her to the cave entrance and stared as she descended the gorge.

Fisk and White meanwhile observed this scene and exchanged glances as Preston continued to watch Parvati and Sanchi walk down the mountain.

Fisk put his arm around Preston's shoulders.

"How are you, my old friend?" Fisk asked.

"How am I? Tired. Often sick," Preston said, still looking in Parvati's direction, his tone of voice without its prior enthusiasm. "The bees and tigers won't let me sleep. But what matter? My work continues. Now I fear I shall be alone, abandoned by the villagers and Parvati."

During the following conversation, Preston gathered some of his paints and brushes, walked over to the spot on the wall that he was copying, picked up his sketchbook and began to paint the area of the wall he had worked on the previous night. White and Fisk follow him.

"We were attacked by the Bhils," Fisk said. "They only scattered when we showed our weapons."

Preston laughed heartily.

"They are a harmless tribe if you have weapons," Preston said. "They haven't come near me for months," Preston said. "Parvati says that they think I'm mad. They call me Tiger Man because they think I've killed one hundred and fifty tigers."

He laughed again.

Fisk gave White a worried look.

"What will you do now about Parvati?" Fisk asked

"What any man does who misses his inspiration," Preston replied, "moan and grumble and mourn. Such beauty, kindness and talent. But she's a daughter and has a duty to her father who overwhelms her with fear of abandonment.

"Fisk, listen to me, her talent is greater than mine and equal to any of the cave artists! If I could keep her here, working, painting, I would, but you heard Sanchi."

"Is Sanchi right?" Fisk asked. "How many people have the tigers killed? Sanchi tells us the white rags hung on the bushes indicate another killing."

Preston nods.

"But there are white rags waving everywhere!" Fisk said. "The bushes look as if snow has fallen."

"Many have died because they don't understand the tiger," Preston said. "I don't know how many!"

White and Fisk glanced at each other again with faces of alarm.

"My God, Preston!" Fisk said. "Tigers, crazy tribes, angry villagers. This is madness! In light of all that, perhaps our news isn't as bad as it might appear. And please, listen to me, as a friend, before you judge. Will you listen?"

Preston nodded, but continued to paint.

"At headquarters they want you to drop this project—but only for a short period—and return to duty. The war against Russia has started!"

"Wars spring up and die like dandelions," Preston said, "while this work is a sacred duty. What good is a painter in a battle?"

"This project too can wait," Fisk said. "The caves will be here."

"Wait? Wait?" Preston shouted. Then his anger ended. "Have you informed them that they march for tokens and trample on beauty?"

Then Preston adds with a tone of sarcasm,

"Perhaps your war can wait."

"You must listen," Fisk said. "They are no longer interested in a soldier copying ancient wall paintings. Your responsibility is elsewhere, your talents are needed elsewhere."

"Images endure but paint decays and disappears from time and the hand of man."

"You've been here nine years!" Fisk said. "Look at you! You've aged twenty years! I left you a young man, but now, now your hair is turning gray. You should stop for your health if for nothing else!"

Fisk saw a scar on Preston's arm.

"How did you acquire that scar?"

"I was trying to help a wounded tiger and it accidentally scratched me."

"How many caves have you finished?" Fisk asked.

"Art is never finished," Preston said.

"This is the last cave, isn't it?"

Preston did not answer.

"Preston, you're still in the army. It's time to leave India. When the war is over, you can return."

White has been walking and staring at the paintings on the opposite wall.

"These are not Christian images, are they, Lieutenant?" White asked Fisk.

"No sir," Fisk replied. "They reflect the Buddhist faith."

"Then why are we so concerned about them?" White said. "Why has the department allowed Preston to remain here at all?"

"Commander Wylie," Fisk explained, "your predecessor, was here when the discoveries were made, and Lt. Preston convinced him that they were of great cultural and artistic worth, created by artisans and monks over many centuries with what he believes are the finest creative talent. The artists lived in some of these caves as sanctuaries and retreats. According to Preston, nothing in their time is comparable in the West or East. If they are not copied, they may disappear forever."

"Do I understand you correctly?" White asked. "Preston is an army draftsman, trained and employed by the armed services to serve its needs. Are you saying that we are supporting him in—?"

"The army hasn't financially supported Preston for several years, sir. Commander Wylie simply refused to recall him."

"So we're allowing one of our staff to wallow away here in the midst of the jungle infested by bees, tigers, a wild tribe called the Bhils, villagers who fear the caves, copying a bunch of pagan images of foreign gods or whatever these images are? Is that what we're doing?"

"Yes," Fisk said, "that's what we're doing."

"And Wylie believed he could claim this as some form of ....what? I now understand why you didn't want to explain our visit until we had talked to Preston."

"Wylie, sir, felt some responsibility for the decay of the art," Fisk said. "He felt guilty he didn't speak up sooner. Pirates and souvenir hunters have already attacked it. I wanted you to see the images and his work. I had hoped that if you saw them—

"Where is your reasoning, Fisk? You didn't think I would find this business ludicrous! You believed that this so-called work would affect me, that we all don't have better things to do than think about some old caves in the middle of India? Art, my friend, will not win battles.

"I'm tired," White complained. "I've made this trip up here for God knows why! I'm sick of India, I'll probably get malaria, I've already got diarrhea, tigers await me in the valley below, I've been stung by I don't know how many bees and other insects, the Bhils probably await again, we had to dodge outlaws and thieves everywhere on the roads, and I'm confronted not with a soldier sworn to duty, but an artist concerned with the work of some dead atheistic monks!"

"No journey for vision is wasted, Commander," Preston said.

"As you wish," White said in an official tone. "But sir, I must advise you, I'm a strategic adviser, and I'm here to evaluate what our role is in all of this. Obviously I know little of art and I'm flabbergasted how the service got involved in this. Now that I have been here, I must say I'm astounded. What strategic advantage could these caves have?"

"They're artistically strategic," Preston said, "like other ancient cultures could have been, if they weren't destroyed by ignorant invaders or those who don't know their truth worth We don't want to be one of those, do we, Commander? Knowledge is advantage."

"What?" White replied, somewhat confused. "Who?"

"Preston feels a certain responsibility," Fisk intercedes. "He and the villagers cleared away the debris, and he's trying to preserve the art for posterity."

"So now it's our responsibility to preserve the ancient culture of India, a land that isn't even Christian?" White asked.

"Preston is convinced that this work is his destiny," Fisk said in support, "that he alone has been given the sacred duty of copying the caves, and that he must, well, be part of them in some sense."

"You look like a pathetic sick creature to me," White responded, "and I'm not sure your mind is all there. It's damp and dark in here even in daytime. And you're living like a wild animal. Have you forgotten civilization? And I must agree with the old fellow Sanchi: There's something eerie about this place!

"Your youth is wasting away, Lieutenant!" White said to Preston. "Come back to us."

"And become important!" Preston scoffed to himself. "And fight wars!"

"Commander," Fisk added, "I don't think he's in any condition, in any case, to join the forces immediately. He'll need a couple of months of rehab."

White motions to Fisk. Fisk and White move to an area away from Preston and converse confidentially while Preston continues to paint.

"Is this the man you knew?" White asked.

"Yes sir," Fisk answered.

"Well, to me he seems mad or going mad," White said. "But then, this all could make any of us a bit strange."

"Not mad, sir," Fisk clarified. "Obsessed."

"How long will it be before he finishes the draft of this cave?" White asked.

"Two or three weeks perhaps."

"Fine, I'll give him a little time, but after that, if he doesn't return, I'm giving the order to drag him out of here. I'll not be responsible for this insanity!"

White and Fisk returned to Preston.

"Lt. Preston, I order you to report to Madras in eight weeks," White said, "no more. Good luck and good bye."

White and Preston shook hands and salute. White began to walk out of the cave.

"I would like to say a few words to Preston, sir, before I leave," Fisk said.

White acknowledged Fisk and left the cave.

"My old friend," Fisk said, "I know what you're thinking, but you must finish and return in eight weeks. I don't want to lose you to this tropical madness."

Preston didn't respond but continued to paint.

"Something stronger than what drew me here must draw me away," Preston finally said. "How can you stand it, Fisk? What shallowness the fighting machine of civilization creates: Does White see the wonder here, the greatness that lies before his eyes, what these artists endured to create this magnificence?"

"White is a soldier," Fisk said, "groomed for war, as am I. He has his own duty and work. As do I and as do you. We took an oath."

"That's truly your concern?" Preston asked.

"Right now, I'm concerned about my friend," Fisk said. "You know that I admire what you're doing, but there comes a time for an end. May I speak personally?"

Preston stopped his painting, still holding his brush, and faced Fisk.

"Your father and mother asked me to tell you they want you to return," Fisk said.

Preston put down his brush and stared ahead, shaking his head.

"Your father said," Fisk continued, "well, you can imagine what he said. 'This work isn't worthy of a Preston.' And your mother is just worried. A copy of Robinson Crusoe in the bag is from her, a weird choice, is it not? I've tried to assure her, but she's not stupid."

Fisk gently laid his hand on the Preston's shoulder.

"I'm sorry. I struggled whether I should tell you, but they made me promise. You need to remember that there are others beyond the cave who care about you. We all want you to return after you finish this work here."

Preston nodded and started painting again.

"Return? Don't you see, I have returned. I have meaning here."

Again Preston laid his brush on the easel and stood beside Fisk.

"Think. What is there for me? That society. Parents whose idea of growth is conformity and achieving what everyone thinks is achievement, who want others to brag about their son, who want guns in the cellar more than paintings in the hall or music in the parlor..."

Preston shouts: "I know why they want me back there!

"...and teachers who love knowledge more than wisdom, and everywhere, everywhere, a lust for the little bags of shiny coins and stones and power. We all scream: See me, see me, see me, see me.

"You know I went to that godforsaken school for my father. I know I did. I went into the army because of my father. Oh, he didn't force me to go, but I went because of him. I didn't marry the woman I wanted because of my father. My mother stood by quietly saying: Oh my, oh my, oh my.

"Compare all that to this. Look at this work, Fisk! What did the parents of these artists think? Where were the parents of these artists when they were painting these walls? Don't you think they were proud? Even if they weren't!"

"You'll be more alone than ever now," Fisk said sadly, "if Sanchi and the villagers live by their word."

"Sculpture breathes life in me, thanks to Sid."

"Sid?"

Preston pointed to the giant statue of Siddhartha, the Buddha.

"Sid! Trust me, the stone moves, the arms use gestures, the face communicates."

"Part of me wants to stay," Fisk said. "If I could, I would share this adventure with you. You know that."

Preston acknowledged him.

Fisk indicated the two bags he has brought with him.

"Some more books and other items I thought you might like. I bought as big a selection as I could carry. There are also the paints and materials you wanted."

Fisk pulled out a musical instrument.

"And your recorder."

Preston suddenly dropped everything and began to rummage through the bag, excitedly looking at the items one by one.

"Thank you so much," Preston said.

Fisk approached Preston, Preston stood up and Fisk hugged him.

"Good-bye for now," Fisk said. "I'll see you in eight weeks. Remember. Eight weeks."

Preston went back to the bags, his head hidden by the bag.

Fisk stared at him and shook his head in concern.

"Good-bye."

Fisk waved and left the cave.

Preston picked up the bags and brought them to his area in the back in the cave.

*

The tour guide entered, a small entourage following, the guide talking as she walked.

"*Now I assume that you've noticed how the styles and techniques of the artists have changed in our tour of different caves. In the early era they paint and sculpt quite simply, with little ornament, almost no symbolism and when there is symbolism, it is the simplest type and with no figures. Indeed in the beginning the Buddha himself never appeared in Buddhist art, and when he did appear, often we see no more than the figure in various gestures, each gesture significant. This accords with the early philosophy of Buddhism, for, we must remember, Buddhism was a reaction or reform movement to a tradition that had elaborate ceremonies and mythology, in which the divine figures were made into dolls. In this sense, in its iconoclastic primitive beginnings, Buddhist art is quite similar—is it not?—to early Christian art, to Muslim art and to Judaic art. However, as the religion grows older, extraordinary complexity also appears, and with it, intricate carvings and paintings of people, Bodhisatvas, animals, plants, and so on, plus, of course, the most complex symbolism. So we see in these caves literally a history of the Buddhist faith from one stage to another.*"

The tour guide and tourists walked once around the Buddha sculpture and left.

*

Preston was once again alone and returned to his painting for several hours.

As the sky darkened, he placed the fires across the cave entrance and set up the lit stick in the wall. Along the walls have appeared monks in orange robes painting the wall and working on the sculpture of Buddha. Preston waved his hands in the air swatting bees and other insects attacking him. He covered his head with a hat Fisk had brought. Suddenly he jutted forward and ran about the cave, brush in hand, trying to avoid a swarm of bees attacking his head. When it seems to subside, he returned to his lotus position and spoke to himself, in a grumbling manner, while painting.

"With its razor sharp sword of convention lunging at me with the force of centuries, history is the great foe of growth.

"Don't you see me working?" Preston spoke to an invisible presence. "Is my cave less a womb than an office or field? Come at me! Strike me, oh friends, family, traditions and customs! The bright lights of me and them descend into the night clay of ignorance and arrogance. Let them mire in the mud of their own thick insecurities, loving their arms and legs and mouths and the tiny things they do with them, locking their potential growth in the traps of recognition and approval."

Preston waited then shouted: "I hear you!"

In a normal volume, he said: "Who can ignore the blaring colors of those hopes and dreams in the forest of opportunity when it is the most trodden trail?"

"In a mocking tone, Preston then said: "Why am I doing this, you ask, why am I doing this, why am I doing this?"

He shouted: "You ask: Why am I alive?"

In a normal volume, he spoke: "The stuff of my being stinks from rotting too long in the sun of limited vision."

Preston laughed and looked over at the statue.

"You find me repellent, don't you, Sid, you of the full spectrum of colors? I denounce black and white and I am black and white from head to foot. I can fool only fools because the sage cannot know foolishness without being foolish."

There was a loud growl of a tiger. The growl startled Preston, but he returned to his painting.

"I have seen the tigers' eyes glistening in the darkness and they have seen mine in the fires of fear, and we discern the same thing: an animal hungry for his food. What gourmets we are, seeing others as no more than a meal, tasting the delightful stupidity in human flesh and drooling for more. Oh, tigers, after you have taken me, romp over and become sated on the battlefields of yonder war, where we, like you, are protecting territory and pride, and are gluttons of property!

Parvati rushed into the cave out of breath. When she did, all of the monks disappeared. She hugged Preston.

"Parvati!" Preston said in surprise.

"Preston, I had to come," she said. "I'm really worried. Despite the protests of my father, the villagers are planning to come and seal the entrance to all the caves! There's even talk of destroying the paintings and sculptures."

"History again," Preston said to himself.

"I can't stay away from you or the work," Parvati said. "Like you, I'm bewitched by these images and I must disobey my father and the tradition. I too yearn to paint them."

Preston hugged her tightly.

"The tigers will not care about your sacrifice, you know that," Preston said.

He held her face gently in his hands.

"Danger begins in darkness, sweet Parvati. Our love cannot trick the night."

"I don't care about the tigers," she said. "I have lived with them my whole life. If that is the will of Allah, then so be it. My dream is to paint like you and become one with these images. Like you, I want to sleep little and paint more."

They heard the sound of voices outside the cave. Parvati ran over to the entrance to the cave and looked out.

"They're here. The villagers are here! What should we do?"

Preston shook his head.

"I am afraid for you," Parvati said.

Preston walked to her, gently hugged her again, then gave her a brush and sketchbook and pointed to a particular section opposite to the wall on which he was working.

Parvati confusedly walked over to the area and began to sketch.

The growling sound of tigers was growing and the voices of the villagers diminished until they could no longer be heard.

*

The tour guide said outside the cave,

"Structure is everything. When we examine these works, we must look for form and structure and how colors and lines are used to make the most sensitive expression. These artists had models. They knew what they were doing. Notice the juxtapositions, the intermingling of lights, avoidance of three-dimensional thinking and depth perception. See how sculptural the figures are."

The tour guide left.

*

There was silence until Parvati and Preston retired from their work and went to sleep.

During the night Preston, laying in the darkness, screamed an incoherent word and then went back to sleep.

The sunrise appeared and a bright light shone on the entrance to the cave. Buddhist chanting sounded very quietly in the background.

Preston, in the middle of a nightmare, screamed out again in his sleep. Parvati was asleep on another stone ledge near him.

Preston turned restlessly and talked to himself, the mumbling grows louder, finally he jumped up, still asleep, and grabbed his gun and faced the entrance.

"Stay there! Come no closer!"

He swung around, pointed the gun, and shot. The bullet struck one of the paintings.

Parvati had now awakened from the gunshot.

"I'm warning you!" Preston yelled.

Preston swung around again in another direction and shot again. Another section of the paintings was damaged.

Parvati ran to him and struggled to grab the gun but she failed to stop him, falling backward. She stood up and hit him, trying to wake him up.

"Preston, wake up! Wake up! You're dreaming! You're hurting the paintings!"

Preston shot again in another direction and again it chipped away at the painting. He reloaded.

Parvati tried once more to grab the gun but without success

"You won't make war here!" Preston yells. "We're artists! We'll not bow to you."

He fired again and pieces of the fresco fell to the floor.

Parvati was crying and becoming hysterical.

"Stop it, Preston! Stop!" she pleaded with him.

Preston fired again and the sculpture was damaged.

Finally she succeeded in getting the gun from him and threw it down the cliff.

Preston collapsed to the floor. Parvati, still sobbing, dragged him to his bed in a dazed state.

"Parvati!" Sanchi shouted from outside the entrance, "you and Preston come down the mountain!"

Parvati, startled, jumped up and walked nervously about the cave, not knowing what to do.

"Please, Preston, please wake up!" she said, shaking him.

Preston slowly awakened.

"The villagers," Parvati said. "They've returned. They're here, with my father."

"Did you hear us?" Sanchi spoke. "We've sealed the other caves and we are going to seal yours. Come out now!"

The villagers were piling rocks and boulders. The sound of their work and the rocks smashing up to each other was noisy.

Preston rose up quickly.

"Where's my gun?" he asked

"I threw it down the mountain."

She pointed to the paintings.

"Look!" she said in tears.

Preston saw the damage to the paintings and the sculpture. He rushed from one painting to the other and felt them.

"The paintings! What happened? Those devils!"

Preston ran to the entrance to the cave.

"Never! Never! I'll never come out," he screamed to them.

"No, Preston," Parvati said, pulling him near her, "they didn't do it. They weren't here. There was only the two of us. You had a nightmare and you, with your gun..."

"What? I?" he said, shocked by her words.

"No! No!" he hollered, hitting his head several times with his hands.

He picked up his sketchbook and threw it to the floor.

"You were dreaming," Parvati said gently, holding his hands.

Preston started to walk about the cave in great agitation at what he has done.

"What kind of beast shoots beauty in his dream, tell me that?" he said. "What dream would kill your dream! What madness brings this madness! Couldn't I see? Didn't the colors enter my eyes? Didn't my joy overwhelm my fear?"

He brushed his hand gently where the bullets damaged one of the paintings.

"How can I repair and overcome what my unconscious won't allow?

Sanchi rushed in and grabbed Parvati's arm, pulling her from the cave.

"Come now!" he said. "They're blocking up the entrance. Only a rat will be able to come and go in a few minutes!"

Sanchi looked at Preston.

"Will you come or will you die here? Escape Preston, while you can."

Preston did not move and was oblivious to Sanchi and his words. He was transfixed by the damage to the paintings.

"Preston!" Parvati cried out. "No, father. I want to stay with Preston. Preston!"

Preston, with his back to Sanchi and Parvati, continued to gaze at the sculpture and the damage done to it, running his palm over the damaged area, shaking his head in despair, tears flowing down his cheeks. He begins to sob heavily.

As Sanchi succeeded in dragging Parvati from the cave and Preston was left alone, the shadow of a tiger appeared on the wall on the other side of the cave, unnoticed by anyone.

The sound of large rocks and boulders being piled on top of each other and sealing up the entrance grew softer and softer until it ceased and then too the amount of light slowly leaking through ended.

"Preston! Preston!" Parvati's muffled and desperate words were heard for a time but soon there was only the art sitting in silence and darkness.

Preston built a fire and sat in the lotus position reflecting and playing his recorder.

The monks reappeared and returned to their work on the statue and paintings.

The tiger growled. Its shadow indicated that it moved around the statue and began to come near the fire, then it saw Preston, turned away, but changed its mind, came closer to him, smelled him, then laid down near the fire next to Preston as he continued to play the recorder.

THE END

Looking in the Glass

As Robert stared at Marcel Duchamp's *The Large Glass* at the Philadelphia Museum of Art, the image of the nude body of Robert's married lover Cheryl kept distracting him and slipping into his thoughts. Cheryl was trying to get a divorce from her cheating husband and her husband was trying to win her back, but Robert and she were in total lust and had been from the moment they met.

'I don't believe it!' he said to himself, 'stop thinking about it!'

The thought of their affair was like a drug.

He closed his eyes and said a few times to himself:

'Stop feeling her body, stop thinking about how you want her, stop the yearning, let go of the pleasure. Look at *The Large Glass!*'

His inner turmoil and efforts to dispel Cheryl from his mind resulted partly because Robert's brain had two other forces demanding his attention: God and Maryanne. Both the seminary life that he had previously pursued before his present studies, and the need for the spiritual in his life, had not lost their appeal. But the image of Maryann, the girl he met while studying at the seminary, intervened as well. "I adore you," he could hear her saying, "because you're a good person" with such "high morals," pursuing theology and philosophy to help people. Maryann did not drink or smoke or take drugs, and refused to have sex before marriage, thus a stable choice for a man of the spirit. But after he switched to his graduate program in music and met Cheryl at a party, he was mesmerized by her rebellious nihilism, love of art and music, and not least her adventurous love-making. Robert started to ignore Maryann, did not return her calls, and made up excuses while Cheryl introduced him to the lubricious sybaritic life, even though he believed that these constant carnal thoughts and lascivious habits of her life-style were not the healthiest path to spiritual bliss; and, yes, he wanted spiritual bliss too.

'Nothing wrong with sex,' he told himself,' but my god, take it easy, boy! And remember, you fool, she's married.'

More than once, he screamed to himself, 'What are you doing?'

When he shifted to his spiritual state of mind, which, without either woman present, was easy to do sitting alone in this room facing *The Large Glass*, at least for a brief period, so easy that the work seemed to make a little more sense; but he couldn't articulate why. Duchamp was an atheist, Robert knew, but Duchamp did believe in some kind of spirituality, possibly theosophy. His copy of Kandinsky's *On the Spiritual in Art* Duchamp filled with notes. Perhaps *The Large Glass* had a group of spiritual symbolic triggers that were affecting Robert somehow on an intuitive level. Unfortunately, he couldn't hold on to those moments of communing with the infinite long enough to stop the flood of images and emotions from Cheryl's enticements and the titillation of her soft and warm body.

The expectation of sharing a bed with her tonight was driving him so mad he couldn't concentrate on the connection between *The Large Glass* and the composer Liszt. Liszt was the topic of his doctoral dissertation and the connection of Liszt with *The Large Glass* was his advisor's idea, not his. Find the link with *The Large Glass*, she said, and you'll have your topic. For two hours he had been looking at it, staring at every aspect, and still he could not understand what *The Large Glass* had to do with Liszt or his music other than Duchamp and Liszt both had less than satisfying relationships with women. Nothing else was coming to him. There were plenty of interpretations of *The Large Glass* and he had tried to read all of them, though his advisor had pre-warned him that research would be of little help, since the interpretations often did not agree with each other. *The Large Glass* itself, she said, was the best way to understand his topic.

'Really? Not so far.' And this was his third visit. 'What was she thinking? What would a work completed in 1923, thirty-seven years after the death of Liszt, by an "artist"—he apologized to Duchamp who hated the word—who only wrote a couple of pieces of music and created very few works of "art" and always preferred to play chess, have to do with Liszt? Who even knew Duchamp wrote music?'

Regardless, he had to come up with some kind of explanation before dinner when she expected a revised view of his topic. Otherwise she had threatened to drop him. What he had written so far, she said, had not captured the true Liszt.

"Do you understand the man at all?" she had said in their last meeting in a tone that would diminish anyone's confidence.

The Large Glass, she warned him, would be the final catalyst.

'Really? This work? This nine foot strange amalgam of wire, dust, paint, foil, cracks, and varnish?

'Let me go through it again,' he said to himself, then repeated the same ideas he had continually mulled over for hours: Duchamp said *The Large Glass* depicts the erotic encounter of the "Bride" in the upper glass with the tiny figures of the "Bachelors" in the lower plate, the "Bachelor Machine." One writer thought the whole work was a humorous exploration of systems of philosophy, physics or mathematics because of the mechanical and mathematical stuff going on in the lower pane. Others saw the "Bachelor Machine" as a conceptual depiction of the punishing of celibates who were frustrated by the inability to reach the "Bride," entering the machine to satisfy themselves. The "Bachelors" of the lower pane were so tiny compared to the "Bride" in the upper pane that it seemed as if many of them were necessary for one of them to succeed in overcoming the devices and reaching the single "Bride."

Robert could feel the bachelors' frustration implied in the barrier between the upper and lower panes, connected only by the cracks caused in an accident when the work was moved. I like the cracks, Duchamp said, now it's complete. Robert had to admit the cracks somehow fit. Was that the universe at work? He kept reminding himself what Duchamp said about retinal art. Go beyond your eyes; see "with the mind," not the eyes.

As he sat there in the last hour "with his mind," it occurred to him that perhaps his advisor was not only interested in an interpretation of the art work, but in Liszt's experience with women and other artists, particularly when Liszt traveled to Italy with his lover, the married Countess Marie d'Agoult. On his Italian journeys Liszt did view many art works, but one painting, the 1504 painting *Lo Sposalizio* of Raphael in the Pinacoteca di Brera in Milan, especially interested Liszt. The painting depicts the wedding vows of Mary and Joseph in front of a chapel. The design of the work, its ideal three-dimensional perspective, and the serenity of its tone were a revelation to Liszt. It so fascinated him that he pondered it for a long time, entranced both by the mastery of technique of Raphael, but also the potent expression of the spiritual. It was to Liszt such a perfect balance of the spiritual and the aesthetic that it inspired him to compose a piano piece, *Sposalizio*, in order to say musically what he felt from the experience and the work.

Liszt's *Sposalizio* was another catalyst for Robert and proved that his advisor may have a plan. When Robert first worked with her, she asked him to listen to, analyze, and write a summary of his reaction to *Sposalizio*. Robert wrote that in three carefully constructed sections Liszt tried to capture the beauty and feeling of a holy relationship. A solemn but affecting, chant-like melody, intertwined with the sighing treble sounds of the Virgin, opened the piece, followed by intricate variations and shifting harmony on the same themes, leading to a middle section of a soft and touching hymn-like wedding march that built to a great triumphant burst of joy in the marital union, until finally it gently ended in peaceful harmony. In effect, Liszt composed a musical mirror of Raphael's design and reverent homage to the holy wedding and to art itself.

Recalling this discussion with her when he summarized *Sposalizio*, Robert then took the leap he thought perhaps she wanted him to take. The reverence and structure of *Sposalizio* were not only an indication of Liszt's respect for the holy event and for Raphael's *Lo Sposalizio*, but of a deep need in Liszt's life for spirituality. Expressing spirituality musically was his way of being spiritual when he could not manifest it in his life. Clearly Liszt saw in this holy marriage painted by Raphael something quite different from his own illicit relationship with Marie, who ran off with him while still married. Their passion and fascination faded when Liszt constantly toured and left her with three children he fathered, two of whom would die tragically before they reached thirty years old, an event that brought guilt as well as sadness for the rest of his life.

As Robert looked through *The Large Glass* thinking about Cheryl and his conflicted feelings—'do I really want to keep up this sexual escapade with Cheryl?'—he seemed to look through it and yet be a part of it in his reflection, he began to connect Duchamp's work with Liszt's numerous attempts at relationships—many superficial, almost all only based in lust—and appreciate why Liszt's creation of *Sposalizio* could be cathartic. Liszt always wanted to be the artist-priest, spiritual and ascetic, but he failed again and again throughout his life, never reaching the "Bride" of *The Large Glass*. Instead he achieved an ignominy that no man wanted from the failure of so many relationships before and after Marie. The flesh would always beckon him, however much its pleasure brought consequences, and he would hesitantly say yes.

Robert looked at a photo of *Lo Sposalizio* on his phone for a few minutes, then closed his eyes and placed its image beside *The Large Glass* and its "Bride" while listening to a performance of Liszt' *Sposalizio*. All of it coalesced. Purpose and technique conjoined with content. If only art could be life, Liszt and Duchamp must have thought, and Robert agreed. If only he could free himself from these feelings about Cheryl.

Raphael's wedding of the Virgin was the perfect model, and the relationship a holy relationship, but Liszt knew that he would never come close to it in his own life; his own relationship with Marie was not pure, not proper, not honest, and filled with more and more conflicts, worms eating away from the inside, a sign of problems to come. As Liszt had studied *Lo Sposalizio* of Raphael in Milan, Robert believed that Liszt realized that the piano work *Sposalizio* was for him not only a music of celebration and spiritual yearning, but also one of regret and then shame, because he could not restrain himself from continuing his torturous needs and escaping the trap he himself had built.

After Marie, Liszt became involved with another married aristocrat, the Russian Princess Carolyne von Sayn-Wittgenstein, but this woman had high spiritual and musical expectations for him, convinced him to stop touring and concentrate on composition, went to enormous efforts to divorce her husband but still, according to her own testimony, Liszt could not restrain his addiction for other women—Liszt had a notorious fling in Weimar while Carolyne was trying to legitimatize their relationship—so Carolyne withdrew and declined to marry him. In the years following that day of rejection in 1861, coincidentally his birthday, in a period when he lost two of his children, with so many signs that he was not leading the life he truly wanted, he finally was able to make a more determined turn toward the spiritual. He took a small apartment at a monastery in Rome, and was ordained. After 1865 people called him Abbe Liszt, his turn toward the spiritual finally taking hold.

As Robert analyzed these biographical details, where the themes of marriage and dysfunctional relationships alongside Liszt's need for a spiritual vocation constantly appeared, Robert had an epiphany. He realized that the themes of marriage and relationships were expressed in many ways in Liszt's work, *Sposalizio* expressing the holy and perfect model of Raphael's *Lo Sposalizio*, themes also possible in *The Large Glass.*

But there were other equally significant expressions. Just prior to the time before he knew that Carolyne would not to marry him, Liszt composed *Mephisto Waltz No. 1*, a piece that expressed the other aspect of his character that had so often derailed his personal life and was clearly not evident in *Sposalizio*. *Mephisto Waltz No. 1* painted a musical interpretation of a section of Nikolaus Lenau's *Faust*, a poem of 1836, in which the Devil performs on a violin to cause salacious havoc at a wedding feast, driving Faust to a seduction that he had refused to do initially but finally relents and runs off into the forest with the innkeeper's young daughter. Once again it was another musical picture of a wedding, but on this occasion, it was not a holy affair. Instead Liszt unleased one of his most flagrant depictions of lust and abandon, an unrestrained evocation of how the Devil can trap men and women with his lurid and bewitching ways.

Listening to *Mephisto Waltz No. 1* after *Sposalizio* was for Robert almost a frightening experience, like entering two conflicting realms of existence, as if he had crossed into Dante's *Inferno* after *Paradiso*. The aggressive, throbbing and unrelenting 3/4 rhythm of *Mephisto Waltz No. 1* draws the listener on an exhausting and out of control train ride, with no relief, luring her or him into a state of frenzy that appeals to the senses, and creates by the seductive sounds and melody a rush of hormonal energy. When played in a true waltz tempo and not rushed, *Mephisto Waltz No. 1* was also sensually hypnotic, like an aphrodisiac under which one no longer knows or remembers what he or she is doing.

The weird fact, Robert thought, as his own inspiration for his topic now came to life, was that Liszt, even in his late period, when he was composing some of his most spiritual works such as the oratorio *Christus*, could not leave this Faustian theme alone. Three more musical interpretations of the Faust story appeared, all called Mephisto Waltz, all different, but all full of conflict, unusual harmony, wild interludes, and strange sounds, as well as the *Faust Symphony* based on Goethe's *Faust*.

Similar to the reactions to *The Large Glass*, which—not surprisingly in light of his advisor's advice to view it—also could be interpreted as a Faustian tale, Robert noted that there were many ways to view the same thing if the audience allows the work to enthrall them.

As Robert listened to *Mephisto Waltz No. 1*, still staring at *The Large Glass*, still looking at *Lo Sposalizio* of Raphael on his cellphone, he for the first time experienced by means of Liszt's life how powerful was Liszt's ability to express these two contrasting sides to his character. With the beginning bars in fifths in the *Mephisto Waltz No. 1* to imitate the tuning of a violin, the Devil magically readying his instrument to play the melody that bewitches Faust and the guests, creating in all a savage need to consummate their desires, Robert saw not only Liszt's pain in never fully honoring any relationship with a woman despite an almost feral pleasure in succeeding in his conquests, but also Robert saw himself on an untamed whirling erotic ride with Cheryl that more and more seemed doomed to end; and perhaps the less stirring but spiritual relationship with Maryann might grow from a different kind of passion.

As for *The Large Glass*, the "Bride" awaited and Robert remained still one of the "Bachelors" hungering for fulfillment that only the "Bride" provided once he had passed the spiritual tests in the lower regions.

One fact was clear: He now felt ready to have dinner with his advisor.

THE END

Bella and the Billionaires

Eight billionaires met at their club every three months to discuss the progress of their decision to create an underground town in case of an apocalypse which, they had decided, was imminent. The facilities planning was a critical part of the conversation—they wanted to be as comfortable as possible—but other areas were equally important. They needed servants to keep up their lifestyle, they had to determine what they would do in the long months, perhaps years, of living underground, but, most importantly, they had to decide who would be the chief executive of this underground town. One town would not need more than one boss. An entire city like New York has only one mayor. Who of the eight would the leader?

One of them suggested that, since only one leader was needed, they take turns every two or three years, but the idea of alternating command was worrisome. That was not their style. More importantly, the townsfolk would compare them, like a popularity contest or an Olympics. Only one of them could take the gold.

Another billionaire suggested a contest. The winner would be the ruler until death, and the rest would be his chancellors in charge of the various departments required of the apocalyptic town. The contest did not excite them, but the revolving leader idea was worse. They decided on the contest.

Various contests were possible, but the choice should be fun, even if it did not work. They decided that each would spend an evening at the club with the same woman, whom they described as "single, mature, attractive, intelligent, and an experienced manager." The woman would be unknown to all of them, her name picked from a jar filled with names of women they would glean from business profiles available on numerous online sites. They would ask her to select which of them would make the best leader. She wouldn't know that she was selecting a post-apocalyptic ruler.

So they picked a name and the potential fate of the post-apocalyptic future fell into the hands of Bella Allegra.

The group of them met Bella at their club and explained the procedure.

"So basically you want me to interview each of you and then decide who would make the best leader?"

They nodded.

"And I would know this after one interview," Bella said, again with a sardonic tone.

They nodded.

"Leader of what?"

They said that they wanted her opinion of their leadership potential.

"Are you guys married?"

They nodded.

"This is some kind of prank, isn't it?" Bella asked. "You have a bet on which one I would choose, right? It's an ego thing, a guys' club thing."

They did not respond.

"Oh, hold on here. I get it. You have something else in mind. Maybe you're telling me this, but in fact you're actually betting on something else."

Again they were quiet.

"Have you done this before?" Bella asked.

They shook their heads.

"And you will pay me one thousand dollars per interview?" Bella asked.

They nodded.

Bella rose from her chair and the glass of wine they had offered her.

"I don't think so, gentlemen. I don't know any of you and I don't like doing things when I don't know what's going on. So, I pass."

She was about to leave when one of them, Ryan, the one who had invited her, spoke.

"Please sit down, Miss Allegra," he said gently. "I think you've got the wrong idea. We're interested in what you think of us as leaders. These meetings will have only that purpose, none other. Simply spend an evening with each of us, at this club, and then pick one of us. Ask yourself: 'Which one of them would I vote for, if they were all running for president?'"

Bella looked at them all with a serious and concerned face.

"Then what?" she asked.

"Nothing," Ryan replied. "You're done. Take the money and go."

"Suppose I wouldn't vote for any of you?" Bella asked.

The eight all stared at each other again and hesitated.

"You must pick one of us," Ryan said, "regardless."

"For example," Bella said, "you already have one count against you."

She stood up and waved her arms about.

"You belong to this club," she said. "I'm not going to vote for somebody for President who belongs to this club. This club is for elitists

and rich people. What would people here know about ordinary life?
And what makes you think I know anything about leadership?"

"We read your profile," Ryan said. "You're a senior manager,
educated, and mature. You have a substantial number of people reporting
to you."

"I still might pick none of you," Bella said.

A surprised look appeared on their faces.

"Look at you," Bella said, looking at their faces. "You're shocked.
Why is that? What have I said that's so difficult for you to grasp? Don't
answer. I know why. Because you think the opposite, don't you? You
think because you belong to this club and have money and position that
people would naturally want to vote for you, because you're worldly
successful, and being worldly successful means you've made the right
decisions, and if you've made the right decisions, then you'd be a darn
good leader, right?"

They said nothing in reply. Her frank tone surprised them.

"Would it be better if we were failures?" Ryan spoke up. "If we
were broke and lived off the street as beggars? Would that make us
better leaders?"

The billionaires all chuckled.

"You can laugh, but I'm not going to vote for someone simply because
he can make a profit or doesn't dress like a beggar. There are a lot of
idiots who lead big companies and wear expensive clothes and they still
can't stop their company from going bankrupt. And then there are those
corrupt fellows who lose millions for investors and jobs for the people
who work for them.

"On the other hand, I'm also not going to vote for someone because
they can't make a profit. We're all beggars, in my opinion, trying to
survive, some of us have just made bad choices, bad luck or have no

connections. The guy I report to right now, he got his job because of his father, not because he deserved it. That's good fortune, not talent or a special ability. He makes a lot of money, much more than I do, but he's done nothing to deserve it. There's only one thing he's good at: acting like he's important. Without me and other managers, honestly, the company would sink.

"I have a theory," she said, leaning forward and talking to them as if they were her students. "If you take that bit away, the bit where somebody gets an opportunity because he has money or knows somebody, then you'd have a lot better situation in every field. Because there are too many geniuses who are broke or don't have contacts."

"Your point?" Ryan said.

"The first question I would ask about someone wanting to be a leader is: how did he get here? Did he make it on his own or through money or contacts? I also look for what my Dad called character. Without character, nothing matters. Look at the doofus I have for a boss. How can I respect him when he has no business being my boss, he has a filthy mouth, gropes staff, and lies constantly? He knows he got the job unfairly, but he doesn't care."

"Anyway, I'm in the dark here," Bella said, opening up her purse and putting on lip gloss. "Aren't you all leaders now? Why would you want me to select one of you as a leader? Aren't you sick of being leaders?"

"We have a project in which only one of us can lead, so we need to find out which one of us would be best. We thought we would find an intelligent, objective person to decide, not someone who knows us or is in our businesses."

"I see. You want one of the little people to help you. OK, so you eight are going into business, but only one can be the president, is that right?"

They nodded.

"Tell you what. Let me make this quick. I see what you're all about. You clearly respect money. Tell me the one who's worth the most and I'll select him."

"So wealth is your criterion?" Ryan said.

"No, that's your criterion," Bella said. "Gone are the days when an Abe Lincoln could be President. Do you really think anyone can run for President without a lot of money? Anyway, I digress. Clearly money's your thing. And it's your project, not mine."

"We know who's the richest," Ryan said.

"Good. Then can I go? I have other things to do and I feel uncomfortable in here. My sister's been begging me to help her choose a dog. Which dog, she asked me, will best fit into her home? Big decision, gentlemen. Choose the best dog. Now that I can do."

Again Bella got to her feet, finished her wine, and walked to the door.

"Fine!" the billionaire Tom spoke more loudly than he wished. "Come back! Fine."

Bella returned.

"Our wealth will not be a factor," Tom said, "though, to be honest, it's more interesting than you might think. Not even all of us earned our money."

"Not surprised at that," Bella said, again sitting. "OK, so let's remove money as a criterion "Could I have another glass of wine?"

"But if you remove wealth," Bella reminded them, "then you can't include what house you live in, what clothes you wear, what clubs you belong to, your investments, properties, and so on. All gone. So what's left as criteria on which I can select the best leader?"

The group became quiet again.

"John Lee is a pretty good golfer," Tom said.

"True," Ryan said. "Yes, we all play golf. So golf. Yes, we all golf."

"Is that a worthy criterion for a leader?" Bella asked.

"I think so," Tom said. "We do the occasional deal on the course."

"So the leader should golf," Bella said, "but since you all golf, that won't help us here."

"True," Ryan said.

"What else?" Bella said. "What have you done to keep yourselves up to date?"

They looked around at each other and shrugged.

"There's no need," Tom pointed out. "We're already running our companies. We have people who do that, you know, strategists and idea types. I think I peeked in on a management training course once, but only to observe the trainer and the course. I wasn't really in the course. Most of us never found college useful. Did Bill Gates and Steven Spielberg graduate from college?"

"Warren Buffet has a Masters," Bella rebuked.

"He does?" Ryan said. "Well, he also plays the ukulele at meetings."

They all laughed.

"You know," Ryan said, "I'm no fan of all these upgrading courses and human resources programs and MBAs and conferences anyway. You can't captain a ship in a class. I say: If you need that to manage, then you don't know what you're doing. Just do it."

They all nodded that they agreed with Ryan.

"So none of you have taken courses or skill development programs?" Bella asked.

"A couple of us have MBAs but we agree that it shouldn't be used as a factor.

"Fine. But there must be skills and abilities special for a leader."

"I can answer that," billionaire Sana said. "You can't learn how to do it through a bunch of case studies. It has to be in you. Managing people, inspiring them, bringing a vision, having ideas, and managing money wisely, they're not skills as such; they're natural talents. We all have those talents."

"Which means, at least to me," Bella concluded, "that any of you could be the leader. So choose by lottery. You're all the same."

Once again Bella rose up from her chair. The group was surprised at her suggestion.

"What? No, no, no," Tom said. "We're not the same."

"Of course you are," Bella said. "You're leaders, you have the same skills, your mindset has been molded for business, and you're all successful. Just draw straws. It's simple. You're clones of each other."

"But this project is special," Ryan said; "it's not exactly a business. It requires other skills. It's more like a community leader."

The others agreed.

"I see," Bella said, sitting down. "Community leader? Hmmm. OK, then you may be in trouble, because, from what you've told me—which isn't much, I don't even know what this project is about—what you do is all you are. And what you do is not necessarily transferable to every kind of leadership. Each of you specialized, didn't you, because you were so desperate to be rich and successful in your field? You may have other undeveloped skills or abilities, but nothing else for which you're trained. Your education, such as it is, has had one focus; anything else has been dormant for a while. You're now, it would seem, brilliantly one dimensional, but when it comes to what's outside that dimension, you're no better than any other manager or worker, perhaps worse because you might find it difficult to adapt. I'm not saying you couldn't adapt, but if it's that different, there would be a learning curve. It could be humiliating. It's like asking Bill Gates to conduct an orchestra or Spielberg to manage a homeless shelter or Buffet to be a school principal. Learning curves are tricky for a new leader. Everyone's watching. At present you can hide behind the mistakes of others because you're accustomed to using others and approving and disapproving of others' ideas and decisions. In a new situation, your ignorance would be exposed, your character could not be hidden.

"Oh, then there's character. You're in that class of people who think they're entitled. That's your character. That may work in the bubble you live in, but in another context, I think you could offend people and sooner or later they'd find a way to get you, and who knows what they would do to get you.

"Anyway, that's all I have to say. Take it or leave it. And keep your thousand dollars. You can pay for the wine. I have to get to my sister and pick a dog."

Before Bella could leave, they asked her to wait while they went off to a corner and discussed her comments.

She waited a long time. When they returned, they sat down and stared at her until she was uncomfortable.

"What is it? What have you decided?" Bella asked.

They paused for another minute, looking at her, then at each other.

"We're going to tell you about the project," Ryan said.

Bella waited and still they did not speak. Revealing the secret was difficult for them.

"Yes? What is it?" Bella asked impatiently.

"We're preparing for the apocalypse," Tom finally blurted out.

Bella did not know how to respond. Of all of the possible scenarios, she had never considered the end of times.

"One of us must be the leader in that time," Ryan said. "Clearly not all of us can lead."

They all waited for Bella to speak, but she simply stared ahead, thinking of the context in which she found herself. Now more than ever she wanted to leave. She was not going to pick the possible future leader of the apocalyptic world. An unplanned wide smile came upon her face.

'These men are sitting around planning the end of the world,' she was thinking, 'and I'm thinking about what dog would fit into my sister's family. No, I'm actually thinking about whether I would use the bathroom here in the club or whether I would go to the one in the fast-food restaurant nearby because it's always clean. That's the choice in my mind.'

Slowly she stood up and shook her head.

"Gentlemen, I'm not going to be involved in this anymore," she said. "I'm not going to select the person to run the apocalyptic or post-apocalyptic world. I want this world to work."

Bella quickly walked away. She decided she would use the facilities in the fast food restaurant so she would not have to see these people anymore.

THE END

A Place to Murder Little Boys

Jefferson Fenwick, Assistant Professor of Environment Studies, grew up in a home overlooking the Don River Valley along the eastern side of the city of Toronto. As a teenager, when he wasn't in school or doing his homework or chores, he was in the Valley, even when the Valley was black, lit only by the areas near the paths and the six-lane highway that ran through it. In fact, Jefferson preferred the night. In the day, the Valley could be busy with cyclists and walkers; or worse, the never-ending sounds of the congested traffic would cover the tender music of wind rushing through trees and animals moving on the forest floor and foul the sweet scent of the forest and flowers with car exhaust.

His parents were tolerant of his hobby. They would sit on the top of the hill in two chairs looking down into the bleak blackness of the Valley and wait for him to come for supper. They respected his secret adventures and were happy each time his form would appear out of dark cloud below and walk up the hill, usually a big smile on his face. Nothing seemed to please him more than his Valley trips.

His fascination with the Valley was instigated by a book his parents had bought for him. Filled with maps and photos of how Toronto once looked, including the Valley, that book seemed to cause some seed within Jefferson's mind to grow. Not only did it inspire him to study Geography and Environmental Studies, but it turned him into an advocate of and walking encyclopedia about the River and the Valley.

He would remind his students:

"People at that time lived next to the River. Small houses, farms and villages spotted the Valley. The residents fished, hunted game, and grew crops, the wildlife and the flora were diverse, and the river had a variety of fish. Where today are those residents? What do you see today? A bicycle and walking path, some manicured parks, a six-lane highway through the middle of it, and the barely throbbing carcass left by a century of mills, industries, and tons of sewage and garbage dumped on the Valley's beautiful face. Yet despite over a century of abuse, the Valley has not lost its inner glory; its quiet beauty will touch your heart and its fall colors alone will lift your spirits and give you hope."

The more he knew from his studies of the Valley's history, the more his affection for the Valley became mixed with resentment and anger, almost grief. He feared he would scream out randomly if he did not control himself when he saw how decades of misuse had harmed the Valley.

Best not to talk about the Valley, he told himself continuously since he was a youth, *stay calm, have a plan, execute the plan, and keep in control.*

For years Jefferson kept busy with the "plan" through his activity in the Valley. The Associations set up to protect the River were too passive for him, too patient with politicians and businesses. Only his students gave him hope. He would take many of them on overnight camping trips into the darkness of the Valley, influencing many of them to become Valley enthusiasts too, and some as obsessed as he. The Valley, he repeated often, was "the most important and beautiful work of nature in Toronto."

*

When his parents passed away and he inherited their home, his wife Brenda Sung also sat waiting for his lanky frame to emerge from the dark cloud, the smell of the woods and wildflowers filling the house as Brenda and he would eat and talk about everything but his activities in the Valley. Now both at the age of fifty-five, she had spent years watching him climb up the hill and he had spent the same time seeing her at the top of the incline in the chair waiting. Like Jefferson's parents, Brenda realized that what he was doing in the Valley was his own secret hobby, not to be discussed out loud. Before she married him, she had tried to encourage him to talk about his adventures there, but he was not forthcoming. Once she asked, knowing how much he respected the Valley, to hike with him along the walking paths. She naturally thought he would enjoy showing her around, but she also hoped the tour might be a catalyst that would allow him to confide in her the plan.

He looked at her with a shocked face:

"Hike? Walking paths? There are no 'walking paths' in the Valley. The Valley doesn't create walking paths; intruders and politicians do. The River doesn't mind visitors, but not when they create permanent scars."

Beyond his activities in the Valley, their life was quite open and pleasant. Every day they had breakfast together before they went to work—she a Financial Analyst, he a university professor—and a supper before or sometimes after Jefferson made his foray into the Valley. They often went on weekend trips, had dinner with friends, and once a year enjoyed a three-week holiday.

Brenda naturally continued to wonder about his purpose in the Valley. She would watch him carry down the hill large backpacks, come home with clothes dirty and backpacks empty, and think: *Where's he taking all this stuff? What could he be doing? Oh well, it's a harmless pastime. When he's not in the Valley, I'm the center of his attention and we're always together. At least he doesn't sit obsessed with the TV or sports. But what is he planning down there?*

But increasingly, especially when he became older, the trips worried her, anxious about him entering the dark Valley alone, wondering if he would return, as well as a comment Jefferson had made to her before they married. Jefferson had told her that one day he would leave her to live in the Valley for a time. He would not leave without her knowing, but he did not want her to marry him without her being aware that that day would come and for a short period she would be alone. Brenda tried to suppress that ominous thought, but on a few though rare occasions, Jefferson had reminded her.

*

Beyond his students, one outsider, Steven Marks, the accountant who did their taxes, did know of his obsession because he also knew of another secret of Jefferson that he had kept from Brenda. Steven had reached a point where he could no longer keep the information from Brenda.

The three of them sat at the kitchen table.

"You don't know?" Steven said to Brenda.

"What is it?"

Steven looked over at Jefferson and Jefferson shrugged.

"He hasn't paid his taxes for a long time," Steven said.

"What!" Brenda said. "How is that possible?"

"Because he wouldn't let me," Steven said.

"But why?" Brenda asked.

"Because of the Valley," Steven said with a tone of dismissal. "I've tried to stop him, but he won't budge. That Valley consumes him and..."

"You know nothing about it," Jefferson said to Steven.

Brenda looked at Jefferson, as if to say, 'Is this true?'

Jefferson nodded.

"He's got some big plan involving the Valley," Steven said. "Jefferson, you may be the expert on the Valley, but..."

"I know very little really," Jefferson replied. "To know what I want to know, I would have had to live in the valley in the eighteenth century and sit on the Metro Council of the nineteen fifties and sixties."

"Nevertheless," Steven said, "that Don…"

"Don't use that name," Jefferson interrupted, bristling at the sound of it. "That name comes from some river in Yorkshire?"

Steven threw up his hands, as if to say, 'here he goes again.'

"John Simcoe, Lord Simcoe," Jefferson explained, saying the word 'Lord' in a derogatory tone, "liked that river in Yorkshire and he thought they were quite similar, but the Valley was here thousands of years before Simcoe or Toronto."

"You're right, sweetie," Brenda said, knowing where this discussion could go and wanting to get back to the taxes, "but you know how these things work."

"I certainly do," Jefferson said with a scornful tone. "The River is unique. I certainly don't think of that puny Don River in Yorkshire when I hear the word 'Don.' I think of the mighty two thousand kilometers River Don in Russia."

"Me too," Brenda said, "and I can say that because I saw the Don in Rostov."

"Canadian Revenue is after him," Steven blurted out.

"But how, why, did you let him do this?" Brenda said to Steven, clearly upset.

"Believe me, I've tried," Steven said. "Why do you think I'm here?"

"I didn't want you to worry," Jefferson said to Brenda, "because I knew you would. And I didn't want to argue. It's quite simple. I won't give them a cent, not until they clean up the Valley and the River."

"Wouldn't I have seen something about it in the mail?" Brenda said, baffled he could keep this from her.

"It's online," Jefferson said. "Or they email or call me or Stephen calls me. They did send a warning by mail, but I caught it first."

"You've purposefully not paid?" she asked.

"Not for quite a while," Jefferson replied nonchalantly.

Jefferson laughed.

"Honestly, I thought they'd be after me sooner."

"It happens, people slip through the system," Steven said, "but not for long. He's been lucky, but his luck has run out."

"But CRA doesn't care about the Valley," Brenda pleaded. "You're only one person. It won't help."

"No matter. I'm tired of seeing the brutal lack of concern. The whole damn world is like this. I must take a stand."

"But several associations are trying to improve..." Brenda continued.

"They're not the government, and I appreciate what they're doing. I do. I belong to those associations. But it's not enough or soon enough. Without the government, nothing will work."

Steven was shaking his head.

"I can't believe you're taking such a risk," Steven said. "Your career, your home, Brenda, everything for that Valley and that River. Honestly, think about this. What good would you do in prison?"

Jefferson had reached his boiling point and abruptly stood up and pointed a finger at Steven.

"What do you know about this? Who's the Taylor family?" Jefferson with a fiery tone questioned Steven.

"I don't know, Jefferson," Steven said calmly. "You mean, E. P. Taylor, the horse racer?"

"I'm talking about the family that contributed to the destruction of the Valley."

Steven shook his head.

"How would I know?" Steven replied. "I'm not up on my history."

"And what happened to Tumper's Hill and Sugar Loaf Hill?" Jefferson asked.

"I don't know," Steven said. "Who cares, Jefferson? The issue here is the taxes. What are you going to do?"

"Exactly," Jefferson pushed. "You don't know. No one knows. No one cares. What destroyed the village of Milneford Mills? Again no one cares. And do you know who said, 'I'll tell you what the Don Valley was. It was a place to murder little boys, that's what it was.'"

"I'm not sure I want to know who said that," Brenda replied. "That's sick."

"The answer to all these questions is first, the Parkway, one of the nemeses of the Valley and the River. And the bully Freddy Gardiner is the one who said it was a place to murder little boys. Freddy the bully was a big advocate for the Parkway and the Expressway. Freddy the bully loved all expansion, as well as whiskey and gambling, but he mostly excelled at bullying the people on the Council. Another nemesis was that group of rabid business people who set up their industries near the River. The Taylors were one of them, a wealthy family that built a lot of industrial polluting businesses in the Valley north of Bloor Street starting with paper mills and the Don Valley Brick Works. They weren't alone but they must be held responsible."

"Jefferson's a big protector of the Valley," Brenda said with some pride, but also with some concern. "He becomes quite agitated if he talks about it."

"And why not?" Jefferson said. "Too few have cared about it since they built Todmorden Mills in 1795. And look at the problems we have with the Expressway and the Parkway. No one on the Council with

Gardiner back then would disagree with my description. Gardiner bullied them and they let him."

"Which reminds me, I must check on something," Jefferson said, extending his hand to shake the hand of Steven. "Enjoyed our talk. Brenda, I'll be back in an hour."

She followed him to the glass doors that overlooked the path down into the Valley. Steven and she watched Jefferson walk down the hill.

"What's he doing down there?" Steven asked. "It's pitch black."

Brenda shrugged as Jefferson disappeared into the darkness.

"I don't know," Brenda said quietly. "I just know nothing you or I do will stop him."

The next morning Brenda raised again the CRA issue

"But you could go to jail," she reminded him.

"No, I won't."

Brenda paused in frustration and shook her head.

"And why not?" she asked.

"I'm going to run, I'm going to hide in the Valley, and, trust me, I know how. I have it all planned. I've been preparing for years. The time has come. Time for the Valley to fight back."

Another long pause brought what Jefferson knew would be her response.

"Can I come with you?" Brenda said, suddenly realizing the endpoint of this conversation and nearing tears.

"I want you too, sweetie, I do. I told you a long time ago that I would one day leave and go into the Valley. I have had this plan from the beginning and you need to help me by staying here. I want you to tell everyone, every newspaper and magazine, every radio station, tell the media online, put it on Facebook, Twitter, whatever."

He handed her a piece of paper.

"Give them this list of what needs to be done about the Valley. Tell everyone that I'm running from the CRA because of the neglect of the Valley and the River and that I won't pay taxes to a government that can lose millions from poor contracts, corruption, and development and yet has refused to help that poor creature."

"Creature?" Brenda said. "What creature?"

"The Valley and the River are a creature, a very battered but still very wonderful and ancient being who lived here long before anyone else and brought harmony with all of the flora and fauna."

"It won't work, Jefferson. It won't. No one will care. If they haven't tried up till now, they're not going to change."

"It doesn't matter. I won't do nothing! I must try. The travesties done to the Valley are inexcusable. I can't stand it anymore. You don't know the half of it! Do you know that they actually shifted the course of the river, mowed down hills, dumped tons and tons of industrial waste and sewage, and…I could go on and on. It's left a scar on that beautiful Valley and the River! I can't help it. People once lived there. It's immoral what the politicians and businesses did. And then, if that wasn't enough, they built Pollution Parkway up through the middle of it! It's criminal. Oh, but they can waste millions because of poor decisions."

Brenda began to cry.

"But I won't see you for a long time," she said. "What am I going to do, Jefferson? I don't think I can live without you. How long will you hide? Please don't. Please."

He embraced her tightly and whispered.

"Don't give up on me. I love you. You know I do. I'm not going away forever. I'd never desert you. But I must do this. Please understand."

As expected, after many warnings, the CRA came for him, but he was not there.

As he had asked, Brenda told every media source the story of her husband. It made the front page of many newspapers, not only in Toronto, but in many other newspapers. The Internet was full of it.

For weeks, the police searched everywhere for him, including the Valley.

The more he remained missing, the more people—especially the environmentalists and those sympathetic with his pleas—became enraged by the situation and demanded a response. The media exposure for a time increased, but in the end nothing was done. There was a debate in city hall and the provincial government about the validity of his actions, but not about pouring money into the Valley. One Member of Parliament said that Jefferson's action reminded him of Thoreau, who went to jail rather than pay the poll tax that supported an institution that supported slavery. Is despoiling the environment any different from slavery? Unfortunately, in this case, the politician said, "at least they could jail Thoreau. We don't even get the satisfaction of jailing the bastard." A large roar of laughter ensued among the members.

The talk shows found disappearance in the woods entertaining, the way they found Rob Ford and Donald Trump entertaining. Saturday Night Live also had a skit about it and made Jefferson look like a prankster.

After two months, an unknown benefactor—it was in fact Brenda's parents—paid Jefferson's taxes and the government relented. The media went on to other news.

There was no reason for Jefferson to remain hidden, but Jefferson still did not appear.

Why not, people asked? Was his corpse rotting somewhere in the Valley? Or had he never hid in the Valley? Was it all a hoax? How could anyone last that long in the Valley without food and water?

The police continued to scour the Valley and kept the file open. But no investigator remained on the case. No one, they assumed, could hide without leaving some trace. Either he was dead or he had never entered the Valley.

Brenda did not lose faith that Jefferson would return, but she was tired of sitting in her home frustrated by her own inaction. Tormented by not knowing what had happened to him, she decided not to wait any longer. She had this belief, based on what had happened previously, that if she walked down the hill into the Valley that somehow Jefferson would see her. She said to herself:

I'm going to find my husband. I'm going to walk into that darkness. I know Jefferson will rescue me because I believe in him. I will convince him to return.

After less than a kilometer of walking around, Brenda sat and curled up next to a tree near the River, shaking and apologetic, then returned home. Jefferson had not found her.

He's gone, she thought. *I'll never see him again.*

*

Soon after Brenda's attempt, each week, for ten weeks in a row, one university student of Jefferson went missing. All left notes telling their friends and families that they were going into the Valley. They left behind the same list of actions that Jefferson wanted done for the Valley.

The missing students radically changed the situation. When young people with proud parents and energetic friends one by one disappear, the police, the media and the university view the matter in a different way. The newspapers now gave it the headlines that a serial killer would receive. Week after week the citizens heard of the travails and the history of the River and the Valley. The police increased the number of personnel involved. The university applied pressure. After three months, no one who read the newspaper or Internet, or listened to television news, was uninformed about the tragic history of the Valley and the River since the eighteenth century. The Valley was the star. The Valley was on everyone's mind. The Valley and the River had suddenly become much more significant than anything else.

*

Shortly after this explosion of interest in the Valley, the ten students and Jefferson left their hiding place and climbed up the hill to Jefferson's home in the middle of the night. They congratulated their professor and went home.

Jefferson crawled into bed beside his sleeping wife and gently kissed her on the cheek. His plan, he hoped, might succeed. After the media exposure about the Valley, after decades of pleas from him and others to rehabilitate the Valley, there was a chance some changes may occur.

In the morning, Brenda, so happy he had returned, looked down upon him in the bed and knew by the sound of his breathing that he was in a long deep sleep. Finally, after decades of dedication and commitment to the Valley, she thought, he could rest. Finally, that great creature he so much loved might receive the attention it deserves.

THE END

One starting point for information about the history of the Don Valley is Jennifer Bonnell, *Reclaiming the Don: An Environmental History of Toronto's Don River Valley* (University of Toronto press, 2014).

Dandelions

On June 10, the moment happened for Trevor Hawkins in a field of dandelions. Shortly before, he was standing with his next-door neighbor Stanley Locatelli a few feet from the place where his blacktop driveway reached his double car garage. Stanley was watering one half of his lawn, the part from the walkway to the driveway, using a silver sprayer shaped like a pistol and a trigger that controlled the water flow. Unlike Trevor's manicured green lawn, comparable to a putting green, Stanley's lawn was entirely and intentionally dandelions, a dense field of yellow. The neighbors had tried to convince Stanley to remove the dandelions and begin again. Stanley refused. He preferred the bright yellow to the dark green not only because of appearance. Dandelions, he told Trevor, had health benefits.

Their views on lawns were not the only differences between Stanley and Trevor. Stanley was a policeman and Trevor a teacher. Stanley was tall and bald with a fat stomach while Trevor was short and thin with a full head of hair. Trevor wore glasses, Stanley did not. Stanley always dressed well, even if he was watering his dandelions. His pants were ironed with perfect creases down the middle, his shirts had not a wrinkle and were carefully tucked in, and he always, regardless of the weather, wore a kerchief around his neck. Trevor, once he discarded his work clothes—which had their share of wrinkles and food spots—walked around in jeans, an unkempt shirt hanging out over his belt, and a smudged baseball cap.

Trevor and Stanley hardly spoke when they stood on the blacktop driveway. The house, the car, the weather, or the street traffic since they shut off the main road, were brief topics, but each quickly dissipated. When the subject of their jobs arose, it generally yielded no more than: "Anything new at work?" "Nope. How about you?" "Not a thing. Same old thing." If there was any conversation, it usually involved Stanley's job, if Stanley thought Trevor might find the item interesting.

Recently the topic was a local young man Stanley had arrested for breaking in and stealing a diamond ring from the parents of the young man's girlfriend. Both Stanley and Trevor knew the family of the thief and had sympathies for the young man's parents. The family blamed Stanley for arresting the young man. In their view, Stanley could have ignored the mistake, returned the item, let the son go free, and let the parents handle the punishment. Trevor spoke as a character witness for the young man—he was once the young man's teacher—hoping his statement would convince the prosecutor to give the youth another chance. But since the young man was a repeat offender, the judge sent him to jail. His sentence was also a sentence on the family since he contributed to the family's income.

But that was a rare conversation. Mostly they silently stood beside each other before sundown staring at the lawns and watching and listening to the hissing sound of the water spray from the hose. They were two figures enjoying their lawns getting a bath. Occasionally Stanley's garage door would be open or he would wear different colored hats and kerchiefs. No matter, still the old green hose was trailing from the side of the house where the spigot was, passed the front of the garage, into Stanley's hand while the yellow vision of his dandelions filled their eyes.

Then on June 10, on a warm and soft night with a wisp of a breeze that made Trevor want to cuddle up to the universe and fall asleep standing, the image of his old self cracked open the shell in which he had lived.

On that evening Stanley was wearing a red hat to match his red kerchief.

"Did you notice?" Stanley said in his treble voice.

"What?" Trevor replied in a low baritone.

"Look."

Stanley pulled back on the trigger and turned around to face a tiny section of Trevor's lawn. He pointed the nozzle at a dandelion sprouting where the lawn ended at the garden in front of Trevor's house.

"When did it come from?" Trevor said out loud but to himself.

"I don't know," Stanley said with a chuckle. "It's the first one I've ever seen on your property. You better get to it."

Trevor focused on the small plant and almost felt like blessing it for its courage, a single life form around aliens, a tiny yellow rebel among the green soldiers.

Stanley squirted a little water toward it.

"I've surprised you missed it," Stanley said.

Trevor agreed. His daily scan of the lawn and garden for every sign of weed, often on his hands and knees so he could see them before they became higher than the grass, was scrupulous.

"I thought I'd let you remove it," Stanley said.

Trevor nodded.

It must have sprouted up overnight, Trevor thought; there was no other explanation.

Trevor kneeled and placed his one hand around its tiny stalk to pull it out of the ground, the small yellow face beaming up at him. Trevor turned around and looked at Stanley who still faced him with the sprayer in his hand.

'Why am I hesitating?' Trevor thought. The stem of the dandelion, he had to admit, felt like he was holding the scrawny neck of a baby.

"That won't stop'em, you know" Stanley said. "They'll just grow again. You have to dig'em out. Their roots can go down quite a few feet."

'I know,' Trevor said to himself, and prepared for the lecture he knew was coming.

"I hate to see you do it,' Stanley added. "They're good plants, more nutritious than most of the vegetables in your backyard garden. You can use them in salads and for making wines. They're high in iron, calcium, vitamin A, vitamin C, potassium, and beta-carotene. They're good as a diuretic, for indigestion, and to remove toxins. The Chinese use them to..."

"I know, I know," Trevor raised his voice, not in anger but in frustration at how difficult it was to remove most of the plant, "you've told me many times."

"Whereas grass? Humans should never eat grass, it has no therapeutic value, none, and lawn grass uses more pesticides than crops."

With one yank, Trevor finally pulled the small group out of the earth with as many roots as possible.

"Let me have the little fella," Stanley said.

Trevor nodded and handed the plant to Stanley and walked to his front steps and sat down. He rested his head in his hands and shook his head.

"Trevor, you there?" his wife called out. "Dinner."

Trevor did not immediately respond.

No, I'm not here, Trevor thought, and smashed his hand on to his knee. The uprooting of that dandelion bothered him. June 10 had begun.

Stanley noticed Trevor's reaction.

"You ok?" Stanley asked.

Trevor waved to indicate he was fine.

Stanley returned to his watering and whistling, with his back toward Trevor.

Trevor then saw an image of himself twenty years ago sitting on the same step and looking out at a barren lawn of grass, mostly dirt and crabgrass, an image that served as a catalyst of how he felt twenty years ago; and an inner sigh of relief happened, as if many weights were taken off his soul, and he for a minute felt independent and free. There were no specific events that had happened in those twenty years; his life had no special crises and tragedies that others didn't also experience. His life was just a life of twenty years. The grass grew and was cut. There were no weeds in it.

Now he looked over at Stanley, clutching the sunny yellow flower that had tried to survive on Trevor's lawn, the green hose coming from the side of the garage ending up in Stanley's hand, the red hat and kerchief; and Trevor could only see himself on his knees for twenty years yanking plants from his lawn to keep it uniformly green, while the man next door whistled and talked of his passion for dandelions. Stanley's passion disturbed Trevor the most because Trevor once had his own kind of passion; once he would never have cared if his lawn was free of dandelions.

A car pulled up to the front of Stanley's home. A man got out of the car, ran up through the Stanley's lawn, and pulled out a gun.

Stanley recognized the gunman as the brother of the young man Stanley had arrested and who was now in jail. Stanley was preparing to seek protection in the garage, but it was too late. The man shot Stanley three times.

Stanley stumbled backwards into his dandelion lawn, bleeding from the wounds, dropped the hose, and fell backwards, still clutching the dandelion Trevor had handed him. Little blood dots and streaks splattered on the bright yellow faces of the dandelions, in some places covering them in red.

The shooter jumped into the car and the car sped off.

Trevor was so focused on Stanley that he did not see the shooter. He dialed 911 and rushed toward Stanley through the thick dandelions. Trevor's heart raced; his breathing quickened.

When he reached Stanley, Trevor picked up Stanley's head and shoulders, held him close to him, and briefly wept. "Hold on, Stan, I've called the ambulance."

Still the hand of Stanley held the dandelion.

"Hold on, hold on, they're be here soon," he said again.

Stanley's wife had also sped to Stanley's side after she heard the gun shots. She took over from Trevor.

Sirens were coming closer.

Neighbors came out on the lawns to see what had happened and eventually formed a small crowd on the sidewalk in front of Stanley's lawn.

Trevor became dizzy when he viewed the clash of the red blood with the bright yellow faces.

He took the dandelion out of Stanley's hand, and gazed around at the small field of yellow in which Stanley lay. From his position on the ground, the field almost seemed as if an artist had painted it.

The ambulance came. The neighbors gave way and formed a corridor through which the paramedics carried Stanley. The ambulance drove away. Stanley—still alive—and his wife were in the ambulance. The paramedics thought he would survive. The bullets missed his heart and other vital organs.

After the ambulance left, Trevor sat there, surrounded by dandelions, holding the dandelion from his own lawn in his hand, and answered the questions of his neighbors of how it happened.

"And the dandelion?" one of the neighbors asked, looking at the plant in Trevor's hand. "Why are you holding a dandelion?"

"Oh," Trevor said, still shaking from what he had seen. "I had just removed it from my lawn and had given it to Stanley. When he was shot, he still had it in his hand and I took it away from him."

"Well, throw the damn weed away," another neighbor said. "No disrespect to Stanley, but we don't need any more dandelions."

Trevor did not respond but stood up, turned away from the group, and walked up to his front steps.

His wife met him and put her arm around his neck.

"It was terrible," Trevor said quietly. "I mean, right before my eyes, with this dandelion in his hand."

His wife reached over to take the dandelion, but Trevor's grip on the stem and roots of the dandelion was so tight, no one could have taken it from him.

He went out on to his lawn and began scanning it.

"What are you looking for?" she asked.

"A place to plant the dandelion," he said.

"Trevor, no. It will spread. I mean…"

"Let it spread," he interrupted. "Let it spread all over the place, as much as it wants. I'm tired of this…this… lawn. Grass is for cows, not people. Let the cows feast upon it."

He found an area, dug a small hole with his hands, and placed it in the hole. The neighbors shook their heads in disappointment and walked away.

Trevor picked up the sprayer and began to water both lawns.

THE END

The Gifford Building

Robert stood before his wife Jennifer and had a decision to make. Robert and Jennifer both sat on the Gifford Trust Board that owned the Gifford Building. Though developers were circling, anxious for the relic to finally die and be demolished, the by-laws stated that only a unanimous vote would permit the Trust to sell it. All except Robert were now prepared to sell.

Once Jennifer stood by Robert and was nostalgic about the old structure. They had plans to restore and reuse it as a clinic for children whose parents could not afford medical services. At that time the building reminded her of the days when it was her family's candy factory. Children bought the sweets with its slips of one-line messages stowed away in each candy wrapper.

That rosy view ended when Jennifer learned that her father and grandfather, John Gifford Jr. and Sr., used the factory as a cover to carry out, in a secret basement area of the factory, subversive plans against any business or government leaders or officials whom they thought opposed their political and economic views. Their only emotional attachment to the candy factory was the slips that John Sr. wrote for the wrappers.

Jennifer learned about the activities of John Sr. and Jr. after an owner of a used book store became curious about a diary he found at a church rummage sale. The diary had belonged to the now deceased janitor of the Gifford Building. He had recorded how he discovered a secret room in the basement, and especially noticed the covert visits of someone he described as Lady X. This vivid description of Lady X was the key that unlocked the real activities of the old man and his son. Lady X was known to and monitored by the secret service as someone who threatened and compromised elected members of congress who had, in her words, "dishonored the nation through scandal and taking bribes."

The release of the diary and its description of the secret room in the basement, and the connection to Lady X, shocked Jennifer, a woman who thought she belonged to a politically and socially conservative family who avoided any hint of impropriety.

Robert tried to downplay the scandal by turning her attention to the building and its many unique architectural features both inside and outside. He pointed out how the small windows were randomly placed around the front façade, alternating with the large windows. Over each of its large windows were molds of intricate designs, each different and intentionally symbolic. Above its main door, whose entrance piece was almost two stories high, there were carvings so elaborate and beautiful that they reminded him of Chartres and Khajuraho. An unusually large diamond-shaped stone sat above the door in the center, encoded with words of Rousseau, with two creatures on its corners resembling part monster, part ferocious leopard, parts of their faces chipped from rock-throwing games of boys when the neighborhood was less gentrified. Of special interest were the friezes of sculpture, on the exterior and interior, story-telling ornamental figures—similar to the bands of carvings on Greek, Egyptian and Hindu temples

Because of the diary, the building to Jennifer was now like a ragged and impudent non-conformist and activist with its tongue out. The long and sleek glass walls of the tall new buildings beside the Gifford were clean and pure, glistening in the sun, and open for all to see, like a tall handsome and honorable man with shiny black shoes in a dark suit. The Gifford Building, with its large heavy stone construction, its monstrous leopards, its weird bands of sculpture, and its scary plots in the basement, was like a short, homeless and vulgar ruffian.

Even worse, when she examined the friezes up close, she learned that they all depicted revolutions: the fourteenth century peasant revolts, the French Revolution, the Taiping revolt, the Paris Commune, the 1905 Russian revolt, and the Spanish Civil War. The truth would have been obvious to members of her family if they had only looked carefully at the building both outside and inside or paid attention to how little John Sr. and Jr. were involved in the candy business. Their business was not candy but plots to embarrass leaders who, in their opinion, were not "serving the people."

Yet, for reasons she did not understand, these images and symbols on the building and the activities of her father and grandfather also excited and made her shiver. She thought how thrilling it must have been for her grandfather and father to be involved in such secret work. Their life was full of risk and adventure. Somehow, because they were family, she had some part in their risk and adventure.

Her husband Robert had no interest in what people had done in the building. When he stared at the Gifford, he saw a beautiful young woman with elegant and captivating features, an interesting and profound architectural story. What was profound about those boring, icy-looking, and stiff skyscrapers beside it? They had no story. The narrative of the Gifford must never be allowed to die, he said, even if it had rebellion within it.

"Let's look at it clearly, hon," he said, searching for another way to convince her. "Your father and grandfather were not starting a revolution; they were trying to ensure that freedom and humans rights would never be sacrificed by corrupt people in government and business. I don't approve of their tactics—using threats and blackmail and so on—but they did want better leaders and a better nation."

"Why are you so intent on saving it?" Jennifer attacked. "It's filled with symbols and images of revolt. Have you thought about what my father and grandfather were doing! Who wants to be reminded of that?"

Robert did not know how to respond. He understood how she felt. The news about her family background was difficult for her. Yet he needed a way to influence her.

His long hesitation in answering was curious to Jennifer.

"Or perhaps you were involved?" Jennifer boldly inquired. "Maybe that's why you're so passionate about this building. Maybe that's why you're supporting them now. You knew my father quite well. You worked with him before you knew me."

Robert stepped back in horror at her statements. Robert knew no more than she about the diary and the work of John Sr. and Jr. But to think of himself as someone who would do such things was ridiculous. Why would she ask such a question?

"Well? Were you?" Jennifer probed. "I mean, you said it yourself. They were trying to stop corruption."

'What would she do if I was involved?' Robert calculated. 'Would it change the view of the building in her eyes? Should I lie or should I tell the truth?'

"Robert! Do you hear me?" she persisted.

"Yes, I was part of it," Robert blurted out without knowing how the words came forth.

Jennifer nodded knowingly, as if she had wanted to believe it. She began to ruminate as she walked around the room, occasionally glancing back at her husband, seeing him anew.

"And will you be compromised?" Jennifer asked. "Will we, you and I, be compromised?" as if she now was part of the conspiracy.

"Not directly," Robert said, also walking around the room, trying to expand his capricious fabrication on the fly. "They intentionally kept me away from the more dangerous work. My work was mundane and could never implicate me."

"But you were complicit," Jennifer said. "Something could be discovered that could implicate you?"

"Unlikely. But yes, I suppose so."

'My husband was an activist, involved in secret activities?' Jennifer asked herself as she turned away from him. 'He's a kind of revolutionary. Oh, my lord, what would my friends think? It's so daring.'

Another shiver sped through her body. The tiniest of smiles, a sliver of pride, visible only to someone looking very closely, appeared. It was not that she had any desire to question, march or protest. Jennifer liked to think about rebelling now and then, but she would never openly rebel. Some small part of her wanted to have the potential to fight for change, without acting on it, of course, and without facing any danger or consequences.

"Are you still involved?" Jennifer quickly asked sternly, turning back to face him.

Robert shook his head.

The face of his wife showed a little disappointment at his denial.

"I wasn't like them," Robert said. "You know me. That was years ago."

'Was the building worth this deceit?' he thought again.

He was desperate. The Gifford haunted him every night when he tried to sleep. He could not wipe it out of his mind. It seemed to be pleading and begging him to find a way.

'But this is my wife,' he answered himself. 'No, I will stop this deceit. I will confess right now.'

"Then we must save it!" Jennifer interrupted his thoughts and said to his astonishment. "We must restore it so that it'll be remembered again both for its life as a candy factory, and for its new life, a clinic to help the children of the poor. The image of children, that's the key. If we destroy it, people will continue to recall it as anti-establishment headquarters. No. We'll restore it and erase any radical memory and give the Gifford a new beginning."

Robert nodded.

"Don't worry, Robert," Jennifer said, giving him a kiss on the cheek. "I forgive you. I'm sure you wanted your wild and rebellious moment. I understand. But Robert, really? What were you thinking? You know we're not those kinds of people."

THE END

The Red Monk

Rachel had begun to hear a call within her, an uncomfortable and eerie voice urging her to transcend her life and fill herself up with a food she had not tasted. The feeling frightened her and initially made her think she was going mad, but soon she began to believe that her condition was not madness but something mystical, outside the normal state of consciousness. The inner call wanted her to find or be something new, as if her real life was elsewhere.

After reading about the sacred sites in India, Rachel believed that India had the answer. Her salvation would be in the holy shrines in the middle of the street, the river Ganges that could purge and purify, the temples and caves that were sanctuaries of holy people for centuries, the profound stone carvings and painted messages on their walls, the monks and nuns who wander the sacred grounds who could guide one to a higher life, and the retreats led by gurus with possible answers to her plight, perhaps bringing some kind of enlightenment.

Her husband Murray frankly preferred a holiday in Mexico or Costa Rica, but he knew that going to India was an obsession for her. In her state of mind, he didn't want her to go without him.

*

The Ellora caves were their last stop on an extended tour around sacred India. They had visited Amritsar, the Ajanta Caves, Kanchipuram, Sanchi, Allahabad, Khajuraho, Mount Shatrunjaya, the Palitana Temples of Gujarat, and Varanasi. After completing this journey through so many sites of supposed spiritual power, Rachel had grown more and more anxious and sometimes sick from the mounting confusion about her life that had driven her to India. Now, at Ellora, she could barely move from a fear that there would be no resolution. Despite this sense of dread, she was determined not to run and return home; she would confront this voice that beckoned.

Murray roamed with the other tourists, amazed at how the artists had carved such beauty out of hills, but he did not venture beyond that observation and had no revelation. To him these carvings were like fairy tales told in stone; they were great art, but art that meant nothing to him because he was not Hindu, Buddhist or Jain, and had no acquaintance with the stories of Vishnu, Krishna, Ganga, Brahman, Parvati, Shiva, and other divine manifestations.

Rachel sat cross-legged and gazed at the walls within the eighth century Kailasanatha Temple, a multi-storied structure much larger than the Parthenon carved out of a giant basalt hill from the top down and dedicated to Shiva. The magnificence of the carvings and sculpture depicting Ramayana and the Mahabharata tales was overwhelming not only because the exotic mystery and majesty of the monumental stone art were undeniable, but because she believed that the art had many stories to tell that could transform her as it had apparently transformed others.

Walking around, sitting on the ledges, or squatting were also nuns and monks in many colored garments. One of them hidden in the shadows in an orange robe had caught her eye. In the Lotus position he sat, reciting a chant she could barely hear. On the ground beside him was a book with worn covers. She stared at him for some time. At least twenty minutes passed while she waited for him to finish his ritual and emerge from his trance. Finally he stopped and turned toward her. When Rachel looked at his eyes, she saw the reflection of the figures of the sculpture in them from the nearby temple.

"They move, you know, and communicate," he said to her. "Shiva not only expresses reality through those tales but brings them to life and guides you, if you are ready."

"What?" Rachel said, somewhat surprised at how he had skipped pleasantries and spoke to her as if he had known her for many years.

He pointed at the sculpted friezes.

"If you come at a certain time, and if you are in a certain state of mind, you can see them move and hear them talk to you in your mind. When that happens, you've felt something of reality and it will draw you into the transcendent realm they represent. It's like the effect of profound music. You become filled up with special harmonic patterns that move you away from your humdrum existence. Art becomes a vehicle for change."

Rachel nodded, not fully sure what he meant.

Just then she noticed another monk in a red robe leaning on the wall with a smirk on his face.

"Don't believe a word he says," the red monk said, "or any of them for that matter. Their spiritual condition more reflects the ruins than the inner spiritual forces of long ago. Most of them are beggars, preying upon tourists, pretending to know something profound."

"Most of them?" Rachel asked.

"Yes," the red monk said. "Not all. Some are sincere, but like this fellow, sad searchers."

"And who are you?"

"I'm someone searching for truth," the orange robed monk said.

"No," Rachel said, "I was asking the red robed monk."

"You see the red monk?" the orange monk asked.

Rachel nodded.

"He speaks to you?"

She nodded again.

"But how could that be? You're a...a...tourist."

"I want to…" Rachel began to speak.

"You want to what?" the red monk interrupted.

"That is your husband?" the red monk continued, pointing at Murray, who was clearly watching her while looking at the temple."

She nodded.

"Does he know you're tired of your life?" the red monk asked.

"What's he saying, the red monk?" the orange monk asked.

The red monk moved closer to the orange monk and sat in the diamond pose directly in front of him.

"I didn't say that I was tired of my life," Rachel said to the red robed monk, "I was going to say that I want to know…"

"Know? Know?" the orange monk interrupted upon hearing the word 'know.' "Is he talking about divine knowledge? Tell me. What does he say about divine knowledge? How do we know? Is he commenting on the Vedas?"

The orange monk stood up.

"Unfortunately," the red monk said, still sitting, "so many poor innocent people talk to these jokers seeking some spiritual solace. Only a very few can help them."

"Ask him about how knowledge…," the orange monk said.

"Tell him nothing," the red monk said.

"I love my husband," Rachel explained to the red monk, "but my life seems so hollow, and I need to find what will cure me of this emptiness, or inspire me, because I'm hurting so much that often I can't breathe. Something inside is calling me to something greater. My soul seems separate from me."

"Interesting," the red monk mumbled. "Are you sure it's not spiritual illusion?"

"Why are you so negative?" she asked. "You belittle other monks, you doubt my experience. No, it's not illusion. I know the difference. It's something quite real, too real, on fire real."

"Ah, reality," the red monk said. "I think you may be burning up because you haven't developed your own reality. First develop that to the fullest, then take the next step. To grow you must carefully nurture your seed. To fly you must crawl out of your cocoon."

"Don't talk to him," the orange monk said. "He tries to keep people away from the temple. He thinks everyone is unworthy. Did he mention reality?"

"Is your real as real as mine?" the red monk asked Rachel as he laughed.

He smiled, stood up, and started to walk away.

"Yes, yes," she said, following after the red monk.

"Where you going?" the orange monk called after her.

"I'm following the red monk," she said.

Rachel chased after him but the red monk disappeared around the corner of a temple.

"You can't follow him," the orange monk said when she returned. "He has no followers. He's a guardian."

The orange monk sat again on the ground in another shadowed area and Rachel joined him. They stared at each other for a brief period before he spoke.

"You're not from India?" he asked.

She shook her head.

"Neither am I. Three years ago, I was helping my family with their restaurant and I told my parents I wanted to visit my grandparents in Aurangabad. So I traveled to India and I lived with my grandparents for a time but only to prepare. Then I began this life, became what you see. I had the yearning and the call and what I now describe as the need for union with the other."

A long pause occurred between them.

"Who is the red monk?" Rachel asked.

The orange monk grimaced.

"Who? There is no 'who.' He's like the creatures who guard the temples. All ye without pure intentions and heart, stay away! He scares people who see him."

"What's he guarding?"

"What's real," the red monk answered, suddenly appearing again from around the corner of the temple.

"You believe?" Rachel asked the red monk.

"No, I don't believe what most of them believe," the red monk said, "but I know what's real. I scoff, I ridicule, I disagree, and I denounce because there's nothing here for them. It's all in their heads. I want them gone."

"But you're in a monk's robe," Rachel said.

"I am a monk. The others I must defrock so that they leave the space."

"Don't listen to him," the orange robe said. "You have a legitimate yearning."

"How would he know?!" the red monk said. "This area should be empty and at peace. Instead these predators prowl around it the way the tigers once did at Ajanta."

"I'm saying you're not alone," the orange monk said to Rachel. "There's a hunger in many of us, a lacking..."

"A lacking?" Rachel asked.

"Yes, a lack of life, of that life," the orange monk said, pointing to the temple walls, "...of..."

"...of reality!" the red monk said.

"...truth," the orange monk concluded, "and that—what those stories portray and give and teach—gives me life!"

"Oh Brahman!" the red monk mocked. "They're just carvings by some poor artists who had nothing else to do but pray, recite, read scripture, carve, sleep; then again, pray, recite, read scripture, and carve, and occasionally eat. For years! They were devotees but few experienced the profound ways. I don't demean them. They were great artists, devotees, but few of them had a grasp of what they carved. They were under the spell of the muse and did its bidding."

The orange monk stood up and placed his face within inches of the frieze.

"I know what the red monk thinks. He thinks for almost everyone they're just carved stone. Yet he's wrong. Why is he part of it if they're just carved stone? Art is the greatest and most profound philosophy and no one can deny what I feel. Each day, hours every day, I meditate and chant and try to overcome the walls that block progress and remove the garbage in my soul. Only before them, here, do I sense progress."

He stopped and turned around to face her.

"That's my quest," the orange monk said. "I have nothing else to offer you."

"That quest has little value for you," the red monk said to her. "Take nothing from him. He's creating it himself."

"But you have advanced...." Rachel said to the orange monk.

"Advanced?" the red monk interjected. "There's no scale of achievement. You're either on land or in the water. The challenge is get to land, then stay on land and not drown in the water."

"But after so many hours and days of contemplation," Rachel said, somewhat in awe of what the orange monk was struggling to achieve.

"Months! Years!" the red monk said. "Who cares? So what. Time has no meaning in this space."

"All I have is one fact," the orange monk said. "I have heard its call: I know that it is there, that there is a realm, an extraordinary plane, and it's expressed in these sculptures, in this place. Here there is a portal, a space, and I shall find it and shut all of the doors preventing my way out. If it's not true, why is the red monk here? Ask him that?"

"And those others?" Rachel pointed to monks and nuns in yellow and orange robes. "They are chanting, reading scripture, and meditating. Are they all like you?"

"I don't know," the orange monk said.

"Some of them are like him," the red monk said, "but others are scam artists. But he's right about one thing. There's an extraordinary dimension. And I am here, and I am real. But he struggles too much."

"You chant, you read scripture, you meditate," Rachel said.

"Just tools," the orange monk said; "but tools don't indicate I know anything or have found anything special. I'm slowly erasing what I lack by opening the doors that lock me out. I'm creating another kind of emptiness, the emptiness inside the seed of the great oak tree that can one day produce within me an oak tree of transcendence."

"Must you do this here, in India?" she asked the orange monk.

"Of course not," the red monk answered. "Do you think reality has a location?"

"Yes, I must," the orange robe replied. "My old life was a life of wandering from my true state. Going back to where I grew up forces me to overcome too many obstacles and will fill me up with what has no depth and was a lie, the garbage of my existence. Why should I try to make that false life work? Why go where I know there are obstacles? Here there is something to find, something to keep me searching, the emptiness in the seed of the oak tree."

On hearing these words, words that expressed the raw truth of her own dilemma, Rachel suddenly broke down, crumbled to the ground and held her head in her hands, covering her face.

When she removed her hands, the orange monk had left. Instead Murray stood before her and the red monk was nearby.

"Oh Brahman, don't listen to the orange monk's words," the red monk consoled; "they're just fancy abstractions that have no existence. He can't articulate any of this. The man is trying, I grant you, but he's hiding what no one does or says. He must transcend the words and the thoughts and the actions. But he won't and now he has a bunch of excuses!"

"What's wrong?" Murray asked. "I saw you talking to that monk. What did he say?"

"Monk?" Rachel asked. "You mean monks. There were two."

"No, I saw only a fellow with an orange robe."

"Nothing," Rachel replied and began to cry.

"What is it?" Murray asked, putting his arm around her.

Her eyes in tears and her face red from despair, Rachel looked at the concerned face of her husband.

"Nothing," she said. "Really nothing. Don't worry. I'm just tired. You didn't see the red robed monk?"

Murray shook his head.

"Whose book is this?" Murray said, picking it up.

"Could I see it?" Rachel asked.

Rachel opened up the battered covers. No writing or print was inside. It was a large collection of white empty pages. The orange monk had not recorded a single experience or observation.

She ran after the orange robed monk to return the book to him. She searched for him throughout the complex, but she could not see him in any direction and returned to the temple.

The orange monk eventually returned and faced the temple carvings next to her. She handed him his book.

By then the afternoon shadows were beginning to spread across the walls, each of the figures on the friezes seeming to glare at her. One in particular had the face of the red robed monk. Rachel became mesmerized by the poses and motions of what she saw on the wall. The more she focused on the face of the red robed monk, the more she experienced an ineffable sense of release and enlightenment, but it was only a quick sensation, as if a door opened, she glimpsed something wonderful within, and then the door closed.

She pointed out the stony face to the orange monk, but he did not understand what she meant. He was already in meditation with his eyes closed.

Murray had sat down beside her, but his eyes were on his wife because her face was slowly losing color until it finally had a greyish tone. It lasted for a minute and then her color returned.

She looked at Murray and smiled.

"Are you OK?" Murray asked.

"I'm fine. Let's go."

"What happened?" Murray asked. "You looked like you were about to faint. Your face lost all color."

She hugged Murray tightly and stared briefly at the orange robed monk, who had opened his eyes and was perusing the frieze and chanting.

"Not sure how to explain it," she said.

"So you're happy we came to India?" Murray asked her.

"Of course. A part of me shall never leave."

Hidden behind several carved figures in a crowd, on the wall with the red monk, unnoticeable to anyone, she saw a nun with a face not unlike her own.

THE END

The Thebes Conspiracy

Therissa and her father walked slowly down the middle of the Main Street of Thebes followed by six others of her peers. The sight of her hometown sickened her. There were sidewalks in pieces, roads once paved now crumbling to dirt, vacant curbside benches where people once sat and talked of their farms and jobs, barbershops where men argued about their favorite teams, store fronts where children once bought candy and bicycled home, all of them boarded up alongside cafes and restaurants where people once met for coffee and dinner in places painted with bright colors now faded, the wood peeling away decades of hope and leaving behind its demon, despair. For Therissa, despair defined Thebes. It left its feces in the dank rotting wood, in the deserted cars strewn on the street like dead flies in a spider's web, and in the so-called air hungry for the lungs of trees that forced everyone to gag when mostly dust coated their mouths and plugged their pores.

Her father kicked a piece of pavement to unload the dry dirt from his grime-covered black boots and coughed from a parched throat. The puffy gray air coming from his mouth after the cough was a human version of the stuff the chimneys of the now defunct town factories spewed out. Glistening sweat smeared both his face and arms and soiled the shirt's underarms.

Therissa, noticing how fatigued her father was from the heat and noxious air, suggested he walk closer to the buildings where there were cooler shadows and less dust. He dutifully complied. At the same time, she signaled to the six youths walking behind her to remain with her and waved to the hundreds of other young people on both sides of the street, all eyes focused on her.

Therissa's group had cut off all town communications, disabling the Internet, radio, television, and telephone, and blocked every road coming into town with pick-up trucks. Then they abducted the town's main leaders—the Mayor, who was Therissa's grandfather, the Police Chief, the Bank President, the President of the local Chamber of Commerce, the County Judge, and the two of Thebes' most wealthy citizens—and confined them to the bank.

The many years of inaction and ineffectiveness of the town leaders had frustrated the young people of Thebes. They decided to act, based on what they had learned from Abraham Lincoln's First Inaugural Address, where he said that the people have a "revolutionary right" to "overthrow any government of which they have grown weary." Therissa and her group—which mostly consisted of high school seniors and students from the local Thebes College—had "grown weary" and planned the events carefully. As a prelude, two years ago they boycotted and "overthrew" Thebes College, shutting down its operation for a month until the administration met their demands. Power was on their side. What, after all, is a college without any students or the monies from their tuition? Now a much greater number of young people had joined to overthrow the Town of Thebes and shut down its operation.

Her father knew her plan and represented the few adults who approved; but even that minority feared what would happen to anyone who walked beside them. Most adults chose to remain inside, behind doors, and not brave the sun and inhale the polluted air. Instead they gawked from windows splattered with memories of better days, all afraid to think of the consequences. Therissa's mother stayed at home, embarrassed at what her father, the mayor, would think of her and Therissa.

*

Therissa and her Dad now stood in front of the National City Bank and Trust's clean, almost new, brick walls, the sparkling windows protected by bars, and a gold door embossed with stampings of the founders and their motto, "Bank here, Gain a future."

Both Therissa and her Dad wanted to believe that they were representing the townspeople, even if the adult citizens did not march beside them. They believed that most of the citizens were afraid to confront the authorities. Many of them with financial troubles had stood in front of the same gold door and always felt like knocking first, as if it was a stranger's house, and saying, "May I please enter," expecting to hear a robotic response, "If you have money or property or a job, you're welcome here. Otherwise, stay outside."

Therissa and her father opened the gold door and faced a long gold table and behind it, in six throne-like cushioned chairs, the seven leaders of Thebes. Those leaders each had a clamp around one of their legs; and extending from the clamp a long chain that allowed them to reach the bathroom. If anyone dared to attempt to leave or enter the building or have any communication with the seven, the conspirators threatened to lock the bathroom, turn off the lights, and play extremely loud music.

*

Therissa knew that her plan had a small window for success. Eventually news of their actions would somehow squeeze through the communication barriers they had erected. The armed forces or police services in some form would arrive and easily overcome them with their numbers and weapons; but not, she hoped, before she had reached the goal. Several from the group were filming the events with video cameras from different angles from the time they abducted the leaders until now. They would then leave town and upload the edited video on to the Internet.

After Therissa and her father entered the bank, the youths outside dragged a pre-built high platform into the middle of the street with seven trap doors and above them seven nooses. Hundreds of youths were surrounding the stage, waiting for Therissa to reappear with the leaders. In addition, there were several hundred more youths in windows, on balconies, porches, and other positions.

"Have you made your decision?" Therissa immediately asked in a quiet calm voice the leaders inside the bank. "Are you prepared to relinquish control to us?"

The seven leaders had nervously waited for her arrival and rushed at her, their chains making a racket, and pinned her so that she could not move her arms.

Therissa did not try to move. Instead her reaction was a wide smile for the camera as it captured everything on film.

"Have you made your decision?" she asked again.

"Now you're our captive," the police captain proudly said. "Tell them to release us or..."

"I will ask you again," she said, interrupting, ignoring his threat and pointing at the camera. "Have you made your decision?"

There was a long pause.

"I have several thousand angry compatriots outside that door," she told the police chief. "Do you really think you can hold them off while clamped and chained?"

The police chief relented and went back to his chair.

"Do you have a decision?" Therissa asked.

"Yes," the mayor, her grandfather, said in a booming, authoritative voice. "Yes, of course we have a decision. We won't relinquish control of Thebes to a bunch of adolescents! This is nonsense. I'm ashamed of you, Therissa. That business at the college was hard enough for your family and the town. But this! Think of your mother! End this now before someone is hurt."

Handing the keys to her father, Therissa instructed him,

"Take them outside to the platform."

"What are you going to do with us?" the bank president asked.

The group brought them outside, each of their chains smashing up against the door and other objects as they left, the sun so bright they covered their eyes. They were taken up the steps to their positions on the platform, the nooses dangling above their heads.

"Are you crazy?" the police chief said, noticing the nooses and trap doors. "You'll never get away with this. My men will be here shortly."

Then Therissa climbed the steps and stood near them.

A chair was brought up on the platform. Shortly afterwards the group brought a man down the street. He climbed the steps and sat in the chair. There was no noose above his head. He had an expression of fright, as if he was about to die.

"This is one of my professors at the College," Therissa said. "It's partly because of him that all of this has taken place, though, I should add, he disagrees with our action and wants nothing to do with us. He would say his suggestion was just an exercise."

The leaders all began to complain at once.

"What will your parents think?" "This is madness!" "This isn't a TV show. You can't just abduct people." "This is a college assignment? Have you gone insane?" "Let us go!" "What's wrong with you? What's wrong with all of you? Have you gone mad?" And so on.

"What's wrong with us, you ask?" Therissa shouted, stopping their comments. "With us?"

Meanwhile the camera continued to film as Therissa spoke to those abducted:

"It's your time, your chance, to explain to us why our project is 'crazy.'"

"That's simple," the mayor said, "you're a bunch of kids who know nothing about how to run a hamburger joint let alone a town. You have no experience, no..."

"Stop right there, Mr. Mayor," Therissa said. "Are you saying that these 'experienced' people up till now have known better how to run a town, known how to makes things better? Is that what you're saying?"

"I am."

"Well, our professor here asked us students to research whether this town, in its entire history, has come close to economic success and has eliminated most poverty and inequality. What do you think we found? That things have become worse!"

"That's not true," the bank president barked back.

Therissa came close to the face of the president.

"Were the road and sidewalks like this when you were growing up? Did you have this much pollution in the air and water? Were all the factories closed? Is the wealth now more evenly distributed? Are the medical services more affordable? I could go on and on."

The bank president did not respond.

"As the professor said, and I quote him, 'the leaders of this town have had hundreds of years of opportunity to succeed in making a viable, successful, and equitable community.' Those are his words. Hundreds of years. Many generations. And...they...have...failed!'"

"This is ridiculous," one of the rich men said. "You can't blame us for the mistakes of the past. None of us caused what you say is our fault!"

"What do you mean?" Therissa growled back, her tone vindictive. "Are you not leaders? Are you not responsible? Were you not elected? You're using the same system as they did, aren't you?"

"You know nothing about the problems involved," her grandfather said dismissively. "Neither does that professor. It's far more complicated. Leave it to the grown-ups, the professionals."

"We've left it to the grown-ups for centuries!"

Therissa signaled to one of her group to place the nooses around the necks of the leaders.

"Can we trust a leadership that cannot even meet basic needs?" she asked.

The crowd in one great voice hollered in response, "No!"

"Can we stand the sight of our town, plus other towns, with so many citizens poor and desolate, with boarded up stores and factories, a fragment of its past, with people who must survive on too little and have no hope, sacrificed on the altar of greed and egotism! Is this necessary?"

"No!" the crowd again in one powerful burst shouted out.

Therissa gestured to tighten the nooses.

"How can you treat your grandfather like this?" the judge said in anger. "Everyone deserves another chance."

Therissa ignored his comment.

"And where else have the people of our town sacrificed? War! The professor told us that there's never been a conflict or war that a leader HAD to initiate. The people trusted their leaders and what did they get? Madness, chauvinism, nationalism, greed, racism, egotism, and...DEATH, the death of young people. And if we do survive, what will the young see when they come home? This?"

"No!" the youth responded with an even more fervor.

"Even an idiot can push a bunch of people into poverty, take away their rights, force them to live miserable lives, and send them to die in battlefields. Do we need such leaders to make us miserable?"

"No!" the youth answered and thrust their arms toward the sky.

As Therissa continued to speak, the youth began to stomp their feet to a simple rhythm. Others used their hands and pounded on the platform. The pounding shook the buildings and riled the leaders. The face of the bank president had turned red and sweat was poring off of the faces of the rich men.

"What wars, you ask? Oh, so many. We needn't look very far. Let's start with the American War of Independence. England started that war when they taxed the colonies to pay for the French and Indian War, without allowing them any say in parliament. Did they have to make those decisions? Ask Edmund Burke, who was alive then and a member of the English parliament. What do you think he said?

"No! No! No!" the crowd screamed to the beats of their feet.

"Absolutely. No!" Therissa said.

"So you think this is going to help you?" the mayor laughed. "You think this is how everything will change? You're so damn naïve. Ask the professor. Ask him if any political revolution has ever endured."

The professor shook his head.

"So hang us!" the police chief continued. "Hang all the leaders! What good will it do?"

The sirens of a stream of police cars, ambulances, and fire engines could be heard in the distance.

"We're not starting a revolution," she corrected the leaders, "we're ending an old revolution that has survived too long and has failed, a revolution that favored the wealthy, commercial interests, the few in power, and those who sought their own interests and not the interest of the people. This town, this country, as Lincoln said, belongs to the people, not to any cartel, institution, corporation, or government."

Therissa signaled the members of the Conspiracy to disperse.

"Don't worry," she assured her compatriots. "We're in no danger. No society can survive without its youth. We the people are the future. We the people can't be stopped!"

In a few minutes the streets were empty except for a few adults and the town's leaders standing upon what they soon learned were fake trap doors. The nooses too were loosely tacked above to a piece of wood. None of the Conspiracy had weapons. The leaders were never in danger.

Surrounding them were no sounds, just dust, a slight wind, a sun that quickly burnt the skin, a main street filled with potholes, the glassy glares of out-of-work men and women now coming out of buildings, and two tumbleweeds making their way down the street.

One youth was still filming from a hidden location on a balcony. He captured, in the background behind the platform, an emaciated dog barking beside the open bank door. The noise distracted the leaders, who turned toward the animal for a few seconds. The dog smelled uneaten food inside the bank, but, before it entered, it lifted up its leg and urinated on the bank's brick wall.

THE END

Donovan versus Donald

Donovan Trump sold an online product called Trumpers, an intangible product of hope, the spiritual version of a placebo. At least that's what he had liked doing and had done for ten years after he had registered a company called The Trump Reality. At first, because he admired Dante, he thought of calling the product Dante or Paradiso—which in hindsight he wished he had done—but he realized that name implied too much. He wasn't selling heaven and the offering had nothing to do with the fourteenth century writer. Then he considered "the Trumpet" because of how that instrument would announce grand affairs or the judgment, and, of course, reflect his name. Finally he settled on Trumper.

To Donovan, the Trumper was intended to be a ray of light, an inspiration, and an encouraging voice to those who needed it; to help those who felt life had conspired against them, and especially for those who wanted revenge on those who had lied to or betrayed them. They would receive the Trumper after they described their problems in an online questionnaire. The questionnaire was multiple choice and the results were quantifiable. If users described themselves as forty, in a divorce, with financial problems, in poor health, no children and how they were betrayed or deceived, the Trumper would say—assuming the user followed the guidelines that followed it—"Your health will soon be better, you will find someone else and marry her (or him), have children, soon have a new job, your financial worries would be over, and those who have hurt you will get their punishment."

Then it would give the nine guidelines that aligned to those (and most) problems: "1) think more highly of yourself, 2) stop any addictions you have, 3) seek help from a friend or professional if you're always depressed or have physical ills, 4) find lovers that support and encourage you, 5) look for work that suits your talents and personality, 6) surround yourself with people who respect you and people you respect, 7) do something creative (learn a musical instrument, or how to paint, dance, sing, and so on) and exercise your mind, 8) spend more time in nature, and 9) smile, because the universe will take revenge."

It was not a sophisticated program and did not have any original answers. Its desire to highlight revenge was again a result of Donovan's infatuation with how Dante describes the consequences of different choices during one's sojourn on the earth. The final two circles of hell were the consequences of those who chose a life of deceit, mendacity, and betrayal.

The Trumpers, like online astrology or card reading but with no mystical implications and using only the information the person offered, were general enough to fit almost any complaint. Trumpers sold for the "low price of twenty-five dollars." A disclaimer was offered up front before anyone filled out the questionnaire as well as reminding the user there was no guarantee and no money back. The final line, in very small type, read: "Here's a link to a free online copy of the *Divine Comedy* of Dante."

*

For ten years Donovan made a decent living between the Trumper and his bartender job and was quite content until a man with his last name campaigned for president. As soon as the campaign began, Donovan was taken to court to change both his company's name and the company's product. Advisors of the candidate believed the website was selling something that was nothing but lies and false hope and would unfairly benefit from the name Trump.

Donovan had no funds to battle this accusation in court. He was not a billionaire or had any extra savings. His family could not afford even to give him a college education and they all hoped that they never became really sick because they could not afford to go to a doctor. His parents and he lived alone in a small apartment on Myrtle Avenue in

Brooklyn, New York, where he worked as a bartender for five years. Despite his low income, his parents and friends said that he should at least try to fight back. He had devoted many hours to the web site. Why should he give up his little business because of a name, a name that after all was his name too? They asked for loans from friends and relatives to help him. Each contributed a little, but they could not find enough to hire a lawyer who specialized in this kind of legal action. Lack of funds forced him to choose legal aid.

On the one side of the courtroom were a group of lawyers and their assistants, difficult to distinguish one from the other in their Armani suits, white shirts, and striped black and red ties, and on the other side, there were two people, Donovan and his legal aid lawyer, both casually dressed. Donovan was sweating and on the edge of shaking. Never had he or his family been in a courtroom; never had any of them been accused of any crime. Now the sight of this group of well-dressed lawyers facing him and his lawyer was so intimidating that for quick moments Donovan forgot that he had initiated the case. Though his lawyer told him he had nothing to fear, even if he did lose the case, Donovan believed that they might take him to jail if he did not win. His head was bowed, his eyes on the table or, if he turned around, in the eyes of his family or friends, but never in the eyes of the candidate's lawyers or the judge. All these people from Brooklyn recognized that this was an arena in which he (and they) did not belong and could not feel safe. The rich were never their friends. It was like ancient Rome and the Coliseum where the slave gladiators, with meager weapons, are brought in to face the finest Roman soldiers or the lions. No, his situation was worse. The gladiators at least had training.

The group of lawyers showed through testimonies and witnesses that there was "absolutely no scientific basis to the Trumper," "no certainty that the person could actually change his or her life by following the Trumper's advice," and through people who claimed to have used the website, could cause emotional harm. The website, the lawyers concluded, was "preying on people's misfortunes" and was fraudulent, even with a disclaimer. Such a dishonest connection to the Trump name brought disgrace not only to the candidate but to the name itself.

Donovan's lawyer responded that the site did not promise to be based in science or to change someone's life. It offered advice. Was the advice unsound? The lawyer used the site in front of the judge to show that there was no harm in the suggestions.

When Donovan, his parents, and his friends left the courtroom, after hearing sufficient embarrassing comments to kill the credibility of his website forever as well as try to make Donovan feel ashamed, a large group of reporters besieged him. They did not ask him questions about him, the case, or his website; they wanted to know what he knew about the candidate. Donovan confessed that he had never met or knew anything about him. What he did know was that he was unrelated to him and that this case of Trump verses Trump was unfair. Then he ended with the cryptic statement: "One of us will end in the eighth or ninth circle and it will not be me." This statement was a reference to Dante and the circles of the Inferno in the *Divine Comedy*, especially the nine circles of hell."

The judge ruled in favor of the candidate because Donovan could make the same living using a different name for his company and the online product. The ruling would also not prevent him from making a living as a bartender.

Donovan complied with the court decision, closed off his company, and took down the website.

There were other similar cases. Not only was Donovan singled out. The candidate's team filed against two brothers named Trump, also real estate tycoons like the candidate, because of their use of the name, but they lost only one of the cases.

It is unknown whether the candidate himself had knowledge of any of these cases, including the case against Donovan Trump.

Donovan's case did stand out in one way. It involved someone who was not wealthy and could not realistically fight back. Many people, including those in the media, noticed that aspect from the start. Picking on the little guy was not the message the candidate had promoted. The candidate talked of making America great by returning business and jobs to America and ending a system that had run the country for decades that, in his view, had taken away the rule of government from the needs of the ordinary working men and women. All these words were cloaked in a promise to improve the conditions of the little man, the worker, the blue-collar ordinary guy and gal. Yet in this situation the candidate was putting Donovan, a little man, out of business for the sake of his name.

*

The court decision did not end the publicity or the unwanted attention on Donovan. Supporters of the candidate came to his workplace not to drink or eat but to harass and insult him in front of the other customers. It became difficult for him to do his job with so many complaints and harsh comments from these intruders. The owners reluctantly asked him to resign.

Losing the case and his job made him visible to the public and the media and neither of them would relent. His photo often appeared as a caution to anyone who misused the Trump name. Media partisans of the candidate now knew about him and even though he wasn't related to the candidate, they still felt that he "knew something" or would harm him in some way, even though Donovan hadn't followed the election and what little he knew was from patrons of the bar.

To keep an eye on Donovan until the election was over, security for the candidate hired Gavin Shackleford, a middle aged, heavy set, veteran private detective and avid supporter of the candidate. They believed that Donovan might attempt some revenge on the candidate. There was, in fact, little to report. Donovan did nothing for several months after the case except sit in his apartment and look at television shows.

If he was rich, he would probably have left the country and started fresh elsewhere. Gavin's reports did not reflect the facts. He claimed to his employers that Donovan was doing something nefarious in his home because of the many "shady" characters visiting him. The characters visiting Donovan were friends he had known since high school, who came to help him rebound from the denigrating experience. If Gavin had simply reported what he had seen and not what he suspected, interest in Donovan might have faded away, Gavin would have lost his job, and perhaps the story might have ended there. But if Gavin had done that, he would have lost a fee he desperately needed to pay for his mother's medical bills. To keep paying his bills, something, anything, must happen.

What happened was that Donovan's neighbors and friends became increasingly angry. They were already upset about the treatment of Donovan, but after several weeks of seeing Gavin, they would give him the finger and shout, "Go home! Leave him alone! We know who you are!" One of them—no one would admit to knowing who—threw a rock at Gavin's car and put a sizable dent in the back door. A group of them then came up to him in the car and told him, through his closed window, that if he did not stop spying on Donovan, they would hunt him down and start harassing his family or friends and continue to damage his property.

Gavin took these threats seriously. He lived with his wife and invalid mother and was as financially vulnerable as Donovan and his parents. Though none of Donovan's friends had the time or interest in tailing Gavin or causing trouble—they all worked full-time jobs and were only interested in pressuring him to leave the neighborhood—these "punks," as Gavin described them to his wife, "had all the signs of troublemakers. I've seen it before."

His wife told him to drop the assignment. The punks could track him by his car license number. Gavin reminded her that his mother had huge medical bills which they now could finally afford. And how would he pay for the dent in the car? His deductible was high and would not cover it.

Gavin did not want to tell his employers for fear they would have no sympathy and relieve him. They would say that they hired him to watch Donovan. If he couldn't do that, they would find someone else. Gavin did tell a couple of his friends on the police force in the local precinct about the dent in his car and the threats, hoping the police might scare them into leaving him alone.

*

Donovan was oblivious to all these events; he sat on the couch day upon day without any interest in what occurred outside his room and with little energy to do anything except moan about the loss of his web site and his job. He had not tried very hard to find a new job because he believed no restaurant would hire him. His face was too familiar. His presence would be bad for business.

There were consequences of his lack of action. Their son's lack of income was forcing his parents to dip into their limited savings to get by. Neighbors and local stores, well aware of and sympathetic about the problems caused by the court case, were helping with groceries and other necessary items, but they all knew that the problem could end if Donovan would start following the advice he gave everyone on his old Trumpers website. Several of the local businesses were willing to hire him temporarily, but Donovan was too distraught to accept and felt too humiliated to be in the public.

The threats, the efforts to weaken him with the show of their power, and the confidence from the candidate's advisors in the courtroom had paralyzed but did not prevent him from being rankled psychologically, as if he was one of those Dante and Virgil were observing. But what, after all, had he done? Was his website fraudulent? Did his life deserve a detective watching each of his actions? How is it possible to continue a normal life if his life—and the life of his parents—could be so easily manipulated? If these people who work for the candidate could stop him from using his own name, and if they could find and harass him wherever he worked, what was he to do? He had no other skill. Restaurants and bars were the source of his income ever since he graduated high school. Those jobs were always public and visible to any fanatic. What public establishment would take the chance of angering a candidate for president?

The constant criticism by the so-called experts in the court soured his mind on the idea of a similar website. He believed his motives were pure, but, he had to admit, he could understand their viewpoint. People were looking for answers and his website could not possibly consider the unique needs of each individual. He now thought the idea was at best naive.

If only he could go back in time and at least have his old job back. Life as a bartender was good for him. He had been like an entertainer and certainly a confidante. It did not go unnoticed that he had the same surname as the candidate. Patrons laughed, asked him if he was related somehow, and taunted him when they learned he was not, "Don't you wish you were?" But that novelty passed away within a couple of minutes. Most customers admitted to liking his open-mindedness and willingness to listen to their woes or opinions. Donovan intentionally took no side, but found worth in every side. This neutrality was not only because of his job—he could not offend his customers—but convenient because he knew too little to offer an intelligent or researched opinion. Religion, politics and relationships were the three controversial areas about which he would not take a side. Of course, those were the three areas most of the patrons liked to discuss.

His apathy, discontent, and lack of energy now were noticeable to everyone around him. He may have stayed in that frame of mind for a very long time if the police did not knock on his door one Saturday morning. In his home bubble a visit from the police was a fantasy. No one ever in his family had a visit from the police.

"Are you Donovan Trump?" one of the two officers asked.

Donovan nodded.

"May we come in?" he asked.

Donovan was so surprised to see the police that he hesitated opening the door, but after a moment he guided them to the living room, where they each took a seat.

"Several of your friends threatened a man in his car," one of the officers began, "and one of them damaged his car. Do you know who threw the rock?"

"I know nothing about it. I didn't see it."

"But you heard about it?" the police asked.

"Everyone in the neighborhood heard about it. The guy's been watching me since the court case. It bothers my neighbors; it bothers me. We don't think it's fair. Frankly, I'm surprised only one rock was thrown."

"We're not interested in your opinion of justice," the officer said, "or if your neighbors can justify it in their minds; we're here to warn you. We've already warned your friends. Tell them to stay away from him. This man was hired, as you must know, by a candidate for president to protect him from disgruntled and revengeful people. He's only doing his job. He can sit on a street for as long as he wishes if he doesn't disturb you."

With that statement of warning, they rose and left.

An hour later his friends visited him and joked about how the police had interrogated them and him. They seemed to enjoy the small dose of danger. Authorities, as they put it, actually recognized them.

Donovan would not agree.

"Leave the detective alone," Donovan said, "the cops are right. He's only doing his job and I have nothing to hide. The villain here, if there is a villain, is not the detective but the person who hired him."

"Of course there's a villain," one of his friends said. "How many people have someone watching them when they're innocent? It's not right. What are we going to do?"

"Nothing," Donovan said. "I mean, you guys are doing nothing. Already you almost got yourself charged for harassment and for damaging his car. This is my business. The cops coming here and warning me made me sick in my gut. It's gone too far. I never had a cop come to my house in my life."

"So, what are you going to do?" his friend asked. "You've been sitting around here for weeks."

"I'm not sure," Donovan said, "depends on whether he gets elected, but I'm going to do something."

In the next week, the bartender at a local bar near his house left for another job and the owner hired Donovan. It was a bar Donovan himself had been a patron. At the time Donovan did not know that the owner hated the candidate and was incensed at how Donovan was treated, how he lost both his job and his web business, and how a detective was watching him.

*

On the day that the candidate was elected, Donovan, spurred on by his friends and the owner of the bar, initiated a revenge he had planned for several weeks. He started another website whose sole purpose was to track every word Trump said in the campaign and in office, record it, and compare his statements to see whether or not the president was a liar, an ignoramus, a hypocrite, or all three. It was called the Trump Report. Unlike Donovan's first site there was no questionnaire and no effort to make anyone feel better or help solve their life crises.

This site was a report card about the president's statements researched initially by volunteers from Donovan's Myrtle Avenue neighborhood in the back room of the bar where Donovan worked, soon renamed the Donovan Bar and Grill. It might as well have been called the eighth circle of hell because Donovan was determined to test out whether here, on this earth, and not after death—in Dante's Inferno—the new president was a fraud.

The Trump Report was not an original idea, but was an expansion of a series of newspaper articles that compared the verity of the promises and statements of the president. Those articles not only educated him about the president but inspired him in how he would retaliate not only on his own behalf but for anyone who had lost their name, dreams, and livelihood.

Within one month of putting it online, the site had millions of visitors, both at home and abroad, and within a few months the Donovan Bar itself became famous for tourists, as well as opponents of the president.

Its notoriety had consequences. In April, a few months after the inauguration, a group of the president's supporters came to the Bar and the first of several conflicts between the two sides ensued and escalated into riots. The last riot not only destroyed the Bar but set it on fire. A tall wooden fence was placed around it and it was guarded by the National Guard. The owner was not intimidated but promised it would arise again.

The unintentional hero of this short-lived movement? Donovan Trump, a man who had lived in complete anonymity a year and a half ago working as a happy bartender making a few extra dollars from his website Trumpers, a man who knew and cared little about the election or the candidate, a fellow politically asleep, the precise type of man the president had hoped to awaken with his message. But the candidate's words were far less a wake-up call than his actions. When actions would have counted most, his advisors brought out an army of attorneys and crippled the life of a little man for the sake of the name Trump.

Even the lesson of the riots did not impress Trump's advisors. Surreptitiously, the government hacked into Donovan's new website and caused it to malfunction so that no one could get past the first page. But their actions were now too late. Nothing disappears from the Internet. No one could argue with the contents of the Trump Report, since every statement was carefully documented and every report was not only on the Internet but was published in hard copy by a European printer, entitled, "The Files of the Trump Report."

THE END

A Hug

In Dwayne Shorter's senior year, two events occurred that brought a couple of rays of light to his dark high school years: He met Elsa Johnson and he played in a dodgeball tournament. Up till then, ever since he was a sophomore, he had to endure the bullying of Foster Dulles and the neglect of his peers.

Foster bullied Dwayne because he reminded Foster of what happened to his younger brother Jed. Every day after school Foster would bring his crippled brother Jed home from the Institute where Jed was learning to manage his disabilities. To reach home Foster would take a short cut across the railroad tracks. At approximately the same time each day they would wait for the train to pass—it was a favorite moment for Jed—and then continue home. On one day Jed lost his balance, Foster was not close enough to catch him, and the train killed Jed. It was an accident, but because Foster was lately complaining about always being the one to care for Jed, Foster believed his parents blamed him and thought he was negligent. He also imagined that his school buddies suspected him; he had, after all, told them that he was sick of caring for Jed. In the end Foster's paranoia about what others believed drove him to transfer to Dwayne's school, but the transfer did not stop his guilt that somehow he was responsible for Jed's death.

"What the hell happened to you?" were Foster's words to Dwayne on Foster's first day as a new student.

Dwayne had several physical deformities caused by his mother's drug habit during pregnancy. Though his internal organs and brain functioned normally, his spine was curved, the placement of his eyes and nose was out of balance, his neck was almost unseen, and one of his legs was shorter than the other, forcing him to limp or, if he was tired, use a crutch.

"I was born this way," Dwayne answered.

Because of his severely bent posture and his eyes always staring at the ground, he had difficulty looking others in the eye. Dwayne tried to twist his head as much as possible, but, despite the pain, he still was looking at them from the corner of his eyes. The effect made him seem threatening and odd when he spoke.

"Do you have any questions about the school?" Dwayne asked.

Foster turned away and walked into the classroom without answering.

Dwayne followed, hobbled into the room with his crutch and sat in the front, near the teacher's desk. He would have preferred to be elsewhere in the room, in the back if possible, but he found that students taunted him less when he was up front.

"We've a new student today," the teacher announced. "Foster Dulles, welcome. I'm sure we'd all be glad to help if you have any questions. I've asked Dwayne to spend some time to help you catch up."

As she spoke, she pointed at Dwayne.

"I appreciate it," Foster said standing, "but I'll be fine."

A few students chuckled at that comment.

"Of course. But if you change your mind, Dwayne would make an excellent study buddy."

The guy next to Foster whispered to him,

"I should tell you: stay away from him in the john. He goes all over the place because he can't see the urinal or bowl. When he's in there, we always separate ourselves from him by at least one urinal."

They both laughed.

That first day, when the teacher tried to pair up Dwayne with Foster and Foster refused Dwayne's help, was the beginning of a pattern that increasingly annoyed Foster. At a basketball game, with assigned seats, Foster would receive the seat next to Dwayne. The gym teacher would sometimes combine them in a duo in dodgeball, Dwayne's favorite and only sport. At the sophomore dance, Dwayne and Foster were forced to work together at choosing the music. In their turns at hallway monitoring, they were on the same shift. The parent/teacher committee sent Foster and Dwayne on a field trip to help in the soup kitchen together. On a trip to New York City, the teachers assigned neighboring seats to Foster and Dwayne on the bus and at two shows. They were on the discipline committee together, which many found especially ironic since no one demeaned Dwayne more than Foster. Another irritating moment for Foster was when the office asked him to carry Dwayne's books because his arm was hurt. Dwayne did not tell the office that it was Foster who had injured his arm.

"I hope they don't place me again next to the cripple," Foster would raise his voice in the cafeteria so a lot of students could hear.

Often Foster would trip Dwayne and then loudly say,

"Stop asking the teachers to assign us together," when he knew that Dwayne had nothing to do with these assignments.

Or he would say openly in class, in front of Dwayne and the teacher,

"Please don't put me with Dwayne."

"I want you to tell the teachers you don't want to be placed with me!" Foster said after he and his gang pulled him aside, punched Dwayne in the stomach and pushed him to the ground. "Do you get it? Tell them! I'm sick of being around you, you freak!"

The explanation for their pairing was obvious to staff. None of the students liked being partnered in the past with Dwayne. Some young people did pity him and would not be unfriendly, but he had no friendships.

The girls were less inclined to refuse study groups and projects with him, but the boys found it demeaning to sit beside or look at him and would intentionally fake being sick when assigned to work with him.

"It's embarrassing to be near him," they would say in explanation to the teachers. "He smells. And the way he looks! Sometimes I don't know what he's saying, it's so muffled."

Unlike Dwayne's ongoing segregation, Foster had little difficulty making friends of both sexes. His tough and confident demeanor seemed to be attractive to his peers and soon he had a gang of followers and imitators, some of whom wrote and published The Twitch, a satirical student alternative annual that, like the yearbook, came out at graduation time and mocked the students, certain events, and the teachers. By the end of his first year, Foster had maneuvered his way into becoming the editor of The Twitch.

With the staff forcing Foster on Dwayne, and the students avoiding Dwayne as much as possible, Foster had been not the beginning but the low point of years of rejection and isolation for Dwayne. He certainly saw no Hollywood potential for his story. Neither a superhero nor a genius, he had never won against the bullies or learned how to do some version of martial arts and impress some gorgeous cheerleader enough to win her over. In the view of girls in the school, he was ugly, or, as one of them said on the Internet, "a creature from some weird planet here to gobble up the human race." No one wanted even to walk down the hall near him, let alone be a girl dating him. Plastic surgery might have helped his face, but no wealthy anonymous donor came forward. With respect to loved ones or family, Dwayne was a foster child who lost his mother to a drug overdose a few weeks after his birth and no one ever established the identity of his father. He ended up in foster care and now shared a room with another foster child. There were no tough guys who wanted to protect him, the teachers were sympathetic but could not watch him twenty-four hours a day, and the final group home in which he lived, though supervised, was no warmer than his school.

Not only did Dwayne take a trip each day from school hell to home hell, but even the walk in between was hell. People stared at him as some pathetic being and wondered how he survived.

But Dwayne didn't change schools or have a breakdown. He struggled on, ignored relationships, and focused on his school work, clubs and dodgeball until finally, at the beginning of his senior year, the universe cleared some of the darkness away. Dwayne met Elsa Johnson, a new girl at Livingston House, his group home. Elsa was rescued by Children Services because of an abusive father, placed in foster homes and, like Dwayne, eventually ended up at the Livingston House; and, like most of the residents at Livingston, for the sake of stability, she stayed at her old high school until she graduated. Each day the bus picked up most of the Livingston students and took them to their schools.

Elsa sat near Dwayne eating her breakfast on that first day of school in September. Elsa was of Swedish heritage and had the common Scandinavian features of light hair, light skin, blue eyes, and high cheek bones. Like many of the residents she had said nothing to Dwayne and had not acknowledged him. But Dwayne always tried with the new residents and spoke first,

"Hello, I'm Dwayne."

Elsa looked over at him, said nothing, but nodded.

"What school are you going to?" Dwayne asked.

"Fairfield."

"Wow, that's in the next district."

"Children's Aid wanted me to stay there. You know how they think."

"I'm at Allen High. Fairfield's our rival," Dwayne said.

She nodded again and said,

"I'm Elsa."

"Hi," Dwayne said.

She got up and took her plate over to the counter. She waved. He waved back.

For Dwayne that exchange with Elsa was a momentous occasion. A young person of his age looked at and reacted to him as if he was no different from anyone else, just a guy. Her words and tone were not cruel, dismissive or showed a desire to escape. She talked to him as if he had meaning.

After she left, Dwayne walked several times in a circle around the cafeteria and said under his breath, 'Yes! Yes!' She did not have to speak to him again. He was going to treasure that event. She validated his existence. Though Dwayne and she continued to have brief talks throughout the coming school year, their first talk was all he needed. He was going to be happy for a long time.

Another key situation happened at the end of his senior year when the gym teacher teamed up Foster and Dwayne for the annual city-wide dodgeball tournament.

Foster immediately complained to the coach but the coach said: "Do it or you're out."

For Foster no excuse could allow him to quit the tournament. If he quit, he would seem afraid to face others. This tournament was also not just another tournament. This was a huge affair for Allen High. Rarely had the school reached the finals in any sport. The galleries would be filled with his peers and others from rival schools around the city, including Elsa from Fairfield High. Foster might lose but he had to make an attempt. His ego was at stake. But why, he screamed to the skies, must it be with "the freak?" 'Why must I be with him in front of everyone, out on that court?'

The gym teacher knew what he was doing. Foster could whip a dodgeball as fast and hard as anyone. He was quick at avoiding throws.

But his success was mostly because he was athletic, not because he had any special gift for dodgeball. Dwayne was not athletic or quick on his feet, but he had uncanny instincts in dodgeball and could not only catch any dodgeball thrown at him, no matter how hard, and avoid being hit because of his bent over skinny form, which was far less a target than others, but he could anticipate where his attacker would throw the ball. When he did throw the ball, no one could guess from which direction he would throw it due to the unpredictable way he had of spinning then throwing the ball, like those who throw the discus or shotput.

In the final moments, Foster was out and only Dwayne and the opponent were on the court. Dwayne had fallen on to his back. As he raised himself up, the opponent was preparing to target Dwayne's crippled leg. That leg always dragged behind the good leg. The opponent threw it as hard as he could at the leg, but Dwayne anticipated the strategy. The throw was so powerful that it pushed Dwayne to the floor on his back. But Dwayne held on to the ball and they won.

Allen High school students burst into applause, pounding their seats and feet on the gallery floor, and screaming as loud as they could. The sound was so thunderous and continued for so long in the cavernous gym that people were blocking their ears. The school was clearly proud. Dwayne and Foster faced them all with giant smiles. Dwayne could not stop that smile for days, but Foster, immediately after the ceremony, was disgusted once he realized the consequences of this win. Forever, in Foster's mind, people would connect him with that "cripple," that "deformed monster," that "freak," and that "ugly thing," words he had used often throughout the time he had known Dwayne.

A week later Foster stood in front of the display of school awards and stared at the trophy of a giant silver dodgeball sitting on a pedestal. On it the names of Foster and Dwayne were forever engraved. Even more embarrassing for Foster was the photo of them smiling on the gym floor, their arms around each other posed for the official photo. They seemed the best of friends.

Foster's first thought was to break the case, steal the trophy and the photo, and throw them in the river. Two problems arose with that plan. The school would certainly replace and re-engrave it, but, more troublesome, a camera that no one could reach and that never slept was focused on the case. The authorities would know who did it.

Foster strategized for a couple of weeks on how he must offset this image of him with Dwayne. After an entire night of worry, he figured out what he would do. He would fix this travesty using The Twitch. When Foster became editor of the Twitch, he expanded its content from harmless mockery to revenge and humiliation against his chosen targets. This year Foster used it to clarify his feelings forever about Dwayne. People would look at it for the rest of their lives and remember it, not the trophy.

Dwayne poured milk on a bowl of cereal and sat in his usual chair. He was looking through the new editions of both the regular yearbook and The Twitch. Both were spread out before him.

He had been crying before Elsa came into the room and he wiped his eyes when he saw her.

Elsa and he had had conversations throughout the year at breakfast, very rarely at other times. The talks were never long, about trivial subjects, but long and gentle enough to keep Dwayne's spirits high. In his eyes, Elsa liked him enough to acknowledge him.

In the regular yearbook, Dwayne was voted "best dodgeball player," and "the guy we wish we knew better." He was in the photos of the dodgeball team, the drama club, the prom committee, the Go club, the newspaper, and the Sci-Fi club. He had made the honor roll enough times to appear also in that group.

The Twitch voted Dwayne "school's best ever cripple," "least likely to succeed," "least likely to find a wife," "destined for the streets," "most likely career: drug dealer," "most likely place of death: in a lonely hotel in the worst part of town of an overdose like his Mom," "most unemployable," "most odorous human," "the man with the least friends," and "messiest urinator."

"City dodgeball champion!" Elsa said, taking him out of his mood. "Think you're pretty great, huh? Beating my school."

Dwayne smiled and shrugged. She had been teasing him ever since he won.

"I play dodgeball, you know," Elsa added, sitting down next to him.

"I know," Dwayne said. "You keep telling me."

"We—the girls' team—we're going to destroy Allen High next week."

"We'll see," Dwayne said quietly.

"Want to come and watch me play?" Elsa asked.

Dwayne did not answer.

Elsa noticed him concentrating on the two books, frozen in thought and not moving. She was curious.

"What you reading there?" Elsa asked.

She quietly moved over to him and read the items on the full page devoted to him in The Twitch.

"Some champion, huh?" Dwayne said, shaking his head.

Dwayne looked over at her.

"OK, OK, I'll admit it," Elsa added after reading The Twitch and trying to ignore it. "I want you to come to show everybody I know you. I'll look cool, right? The City Champion there, watching me?"

Still Dwayne did not respond.

"I look really good in shorts too," Elsa added, giggling, then punched him in the arm.

After he continued to stare at The Twitch, Elsa did not talk for a long minute until her face suddenly turned sad and she sat down next to him.

"We're not like other people, Dwayne," she spoke softly, a pain in her voice, "inside, we have hurt, deep hurt. You know that. Others don't see it."

"Yeah," Dwayne said.

"Take me. I don't like guys touching me. I can't have a boyfriend. And I don't think it's going to go away, ever."

"I'm sorry, Elsa."

"No one talks like this about me," Elsa said, pointing at The Twitch, "but I talk about myself that way, all the time."

Dwayne twisted his neck and his head farther than he had ever done before so he could see her face to face through his still red eyes. His neck hurt to do it, but he wanted his eyes to meet her eyes and he wanted to show sympathy for her with those eyes. A tear came down his cheeks, not for him, but for her, and she knew it.

Then she did what no one had ever done.

She gave him a long hug.

He closed his eyes and enjoyed that innocent moment of warmth and placed it in a special space in his mind, that space where he could go and find comfort for the rest of his life. That hug was now the most amazing event of his life, enough to keep him whole until his days were over.

"That's for being a champion," she said.

"OK, OK, I'll come see you!" Dwayne said, breaking the mood.

"Wouldn't it be cool," Elsa said, "if I won and we were both were champions?"

"Yes, it would be cool," Dwayne said, but not for him and not because of his own victory in dodgeball. How could his partnership with Foster ever be thought a championship?

Her hug was his championship.

What would be wonderful, if Elsa won, would be if Elsa allowed him to hug her. Now that would be so wonderful. It would be the first time a girl wanted him to hug her.

Then, as if she read his thoughts, Elsa said the impossible,

"And if I win, would you give me a hug?"

Wayne nodded. Life, he thought, was good.

THE END

Quest for Fulfillment

Kisha was the spark that lit up the dead scrap of wood that was the work life of three young men. She was like a goddess and they were her worshippers. Not only was Kisha beautiful and alluring to them, but Kisha came from India. That quality gave her a mystique that made her even more attractive.

No one in the office questioned Kisha's beauty, but few understood that in Brahmanism and to a reader of its sacred writings the gift of physical beauty had other implications. Her parents taught Kisha this truth when she was very young.

"Krishna has looked kindly upon you," her mother said, "and transformed you and said, 'I shall show how good is also beautiful. And if anyone asks Kisha about her beauty, Kisha will say, Krishna shows how beautiful good is, Krishna cares about me.'"

So when strangers or people at the office complimented her, Kisha would think about what her mother said and say: "Krishna cares for me."

Her beauty was not her property; Krishna owned it.

None of this spiritual understanding was in the minds of the three young men. Their unrequited obsession over Kisha may have continued until their hair became gray, but a change happened when Kisha hired Taya. Taya was also from India and like Kisha had studied the sacred writings. Immediately this common ground between them yielded a friendship that the trio of young men envied but also welcomed. Now they had someone who might tell them more about Kisha.

Taya told them that Kisha was an only child, had moved to the West from India when her father accepted a position as Professor of

Sanskrit and Pali. She came from a traditional Hindu family, graduated from university in World Religions, and from a very early age learned Sanskrit and Pali and read the Indian spiritual classics. Taya did not tell them that Kisha not only believed in but yearned to live in the great sagas of India. Not a day in her life passed without hearing or reading one of these tales and the recitation of various meditative prayers. Reproductions of the great cave paintings and temple sculpture lined her bedroom. While the three young men were fantasizing about her, Kisha was thinking of a way to be at one with the infinite. She ignored not only the stares of the young men who faced her, but anything that did not fit within her profound yearning.

Time passed for the three young men, but time did not end frustration. Though Kisha did nothing to encourage them in the fulfillment of their fantasies, and remained as demure and kind as ever, modestly dressing and speaking, her existence absorbed their minds. Indeed, the more unlikely the seduction of Kisha appeared, the more they wanted her.

Eventually their minds could not confine the fire of their needs. Something had to be done. They were burning up inside with insatiable longings. Looking was no longer enough. Instinct was hardening their resolve. They must find a way to have her. Week after week, they schemed and concocted plans to snare her, as a hunter would strategize the kill, searching for the best plan to trap the animal. Like animals themselves, they panted with expectation of what the capture would be like. Kisha was beautiful; they wanted to see and touch this beauty in its raw nude form. One of them, if not all of them, had to have her. Among many ideas, some of them outrageous and a few criminal, one especially continued to excite them: to drug her with an aphrodisiac.

Meanwhile, Taya's relationship with Kisha had continued and he had even gone to Kisha's house for dinner. The young men wanted to know everything that happened. Their questions became more bold and intrusive.

"Did you sleep with her? Have you seen her naked form?"

Taya denied any such thoughts and found their probing disgusting. To think of Kisha in that way, he said, was not only ridiculous but disrespectful. Kisha and he were good friends, no more. There would be no romance or intimacy. Kisha sought a higher fulfillment.

When they listened to these reports, they ignored Taya's comments about the kind of woman Kisha was and heard only that Taya was not interested in her. They then confessed their salacious desires and plan to Taya, hoping he might help.

Taya became angry. 'How stupid and obsessed are these men! What demons must drive them?'

He told them in a harsh tone that he could not betray his friendship with her.

Like three little boys who cannot have what they want, one threw a book to the floor, another smashed his fist on the table, and the third hit his forehead with his hand.

Taya observed this adolescent behavior and began to worry, especially in light of their plan to use an aphrodisiac, that they might one day revenge their unreciprocated feelings on Kisha in a violent way. Clearly their obsession was not diminishing. Taya decided on saving Kisha from any potential danger from these men.

Taya first tried what he hoped would be a kind of therapy, an intervention. He encouraged the young men to talk about their irrational pursuit and to share their inner hidden passions with others, though their associates were not blind to their yearnings for Kisha. As the weeks went on, Taya slowly included all the men in the office in the secret of the three young men and some of the women. It was not long before everyone including Kisha knew to what degree the three young men craved her.

Their lubricious feelings for Kisha did not affect Kisha. Calmly she excused their behavior. They were just three males who liked her. So what? Males lust after females and females lust after males. At least these men do not hide behind their thoughts and pretend otherwise. That they desire her is the way of the world. They were harmless, she said to Taya, please don't embarrass them.

But they did worry Taya. The exposure and discussion of their desires to the office had not changed the attitude of the young men. They remained as determined as ever to entrap her.

Taya decided to try another solution. He told the young men that he would now "guide them to fulfillment."

Taya's sudden willingness confused them.

"Why?" they asked, bewildered. "We thought she and you were friends. We thought you told us she was uninterested. We thought you said we were disrespectful. You've told this to the entire office."

"She will still be my friend," he assured, "and you all will receive what you want, trust me."

Had their inner demons not clouded their minds, they might have questioned more Taya's willingness to help them. Instead, as Taya spoke, they had already begun to envision in their minds the delights that they believed would come. They flushed with excitement. Their nerves quivered with the possibility.

The day of seduction came. Everyone met at Taya's apartment and Taya prepared the aphrodisiac. After Taya had given it to them, Taya excused himself, left, but sat outside the door of his apartment. Taya did not tell them that he had also added certain psychedelic drugs to the aphrodisiac.

The three young men sat on the floor in a row, their backs up against the wall, waiting for the drugs to show its effects. They kept their eyes fixed on Kisha, who sat on a stool facing them across the room. Soon the drug was working and they began to watch the walls, lights, and Kisha contort and change. Then for a few seconds they lost their vision and saw nothing but swirls of color. When their vision returned, it was not as clear as before, but they could see in the blur that Kisha had begun slowly to remove her clothes before the hungry eyes of the three young men. Their hearts beat rapidly as they glimpsed each new view of her flesh. It was exactly as they had imagined it. There, before them, what they had desired for so long, there stood Kisha fully revealed. She was just as they imagined.

Her skin was pure and soft without blemish or lumps. She had a smile that radiated with invitation and eyes that glinted with happiness. Long sleek arms fell to her sides with the motion of a sculpture in harmony. Her breasts were round and firm and her pelvic area spread wondrously out from a tiny waist. There she was. Kisha the Woman, the perfect Yakshi, stood before them, her one hip cocked, her eyes half shut, her mouth open, stroking her hair. Even though one force in them yearned to rush at her and enjoy her, another force needed only to look at and worship her.

The first force was unable to resist. They finally rushed at her and, as she stood without moving, the trio turned into one creature, their six hands were on her form all at once, softly feeling that skin they had so much wanted to hold and caress. They were gentle, even reverent, because they did not want to hurt her and mar a single cell of her skin. Kisha did not seem to resist. The experience was perfect, exactly as they had wanted it, as they had fantasized so often. It was ecstasy.

Kisha became as still as a statue.

Then they carried her to the bed and prepared to complete their desires. But before they did, Kisha's head—her body moist, her hair wet—turned into the head of a bull. The young men sprang off the bed in horror and moved back to the wall.

Kisha with the bull's head rushed at them with an amazing strength and speed. "Come at me," she sang in a melody that sounded like a chant. "Rise upon me!" she sang again. The bull snorted and roared. They tried to avoid the head and see only her body, but it was impossible. They could not come at and rise upon that head, however voluptuous the body appeared. They ran to the door to escape, but the door would not open. Naked, shivering, they stood with their backs up against the wall, nowhere to go, whimpering for help from fear.

They each shook their head to erase the image of the head. At the same time, the bull was charging at one then the other, each of them still screaming in hysteria and banging on the walls and door. They also sensed that their noses were growing with scales and had an offensive smell, fluid spewing from them, each looking like a tiny elephant's trunk.

The bull then pulled enormous scissors from under the bed. The three huddled together in a corner, shaking and terrified by the scissors.

The bull closed and opened the scissors in rapid motion until the scissors transformed into a bright disk with a dark swirling pit in the center, ready to swallow anything near it. Spinning ever so quickly and shining like the sun itself, it mesmerized the boys. The bull flung it first at the bed and in one swift motion sawed it in half. Then it (how could they think of this monster as a woman?) threw the disk into the room and slowly it moved about the room, constantly threatening the boys with a sucking sound.

When it released the disk, the bull began to grow more arms, and each pair of its arms began to create and release tiny duplicates of Kisha the size of a large beetles with the head of Kisha. These little Kishas started to scurry to the young men, who were now seated frozen in astonishment, paralyzed, their mouths open and their back up against the wall. The bull created numerous Kisha mites, who eventually reached the boys and clambered over every area of their bodies until they covered them from neck to feet. The boys tried without success to brush the

Kishas away, but there were too many and each seemed to have a clinging power beyond their size. Eventually the young men's energy was spent. Helplessly they sat while the mites with tiny bites began to nibble on their skin.

Kisha herself had a different experience from the potion Taya had given her—with the permission of her parents and herself. Her yearnings were spiritual. She wanted to have a sacred union with infinite powers. Immediately, when focusing on the three young men, she fell into a profound rapture in which the three youths transformed into Shiva, Brahma and Vishnu, the trinity of Hinduism; and Kisha became in her reverie Sarasvati, Lakshmi and Kali, the consorts of Brahma, Vishnu, and Shiva. The union was a spiritual union in which she lost her identity and became enlightened by these powers of the universe as she opened up her heart and revealed her love for them all. The ecstasy was not physical but contemplative and ineffable for the deeply pious and virtuous woman.

When Taya returned, he found the three young men against the wall, their bodies pale and cold with sores everywhere. On the floor in front of the bed he saw his scissors and silver pizza pan. The eyes of the young men were abnormally large and fixed on some unknown object, as if hypnotized.

Taya shook them repeatedly. Finally, they stirred, came to their feet, dressed and, without speaking, left.

The young men spent the next two weeks at home in their apartments. Physically they were sore and were applying continuously a healing ointment to their bodies, but mentally they were even more injured. Since that event, the images of the bull, the mites and the disk now haunted them, harassing them with nightmarish attacks that disturbed their sleep.

Their minds were very unclear about what happened, uncertain if what they had hoped would happen did happen. Physically no sign now remained. They had no memory of any pleasure. The sores on their skins were a mystery. Yet something had happened, some physical reaction had taken place, but their minds left no conscious, clear, and real proof of how it happened.

Back at work they sat as always facing Kisha, more radiant than ever, who smiled at them when they sat down, and kindly welcomed them back.

They smiled back.

All of the fellow workers, including Taya, gathered at lunch around the trio to hear the news, but the three did not want to speak about Kisha. After the bewildering images and their shadowy sense of the event, what, they thought, could they say to their colleagues?

In Kisha, they saw a glow of fulfillment beaming all over her face for no reason known to them. How can she look so serene and they feel so confused? Did she not know what happened? That question itself disturbed them, because their own experience was uncertain. They knew she had been there, but they expected to see her differently or knowingly. Now she looked at them as if they had never met outside work. They themselves had no feeling or memory of touching her body and no images of seeing her beautiful form. Yet they were there. After all, there was not one but three of them as witnesses.

"We don't want to talk about it!" the trio insisted to their peers.

"Why, what happened?" the other men wondered.

"What does it matter?" the trio responded with a tone of irritation. "Leave us alone!"

The other men shook their heads, disappointed, and returned to their desks.

After the others had left, Taya looked over at the trio and smiled.

"I wouldn't have believed it," Taya said, "but you fellows are gentlemen. You didn't make up some story. That was a kind thing to do."

They did not reply, but thought: 'What story could they create? They had no memory of what really happened.'

That afternoon, just before they were leaving work for home, they overheard Taya and Kisha talking in the cafeteria area.

Kisha was enthusiastic.

"Oh, Taya," she whispered, "how can I thank you? It was as you said. Father is so proud. It happened just as I hoped. I'm so happy. I go over it again and again in detail just to be certain, and he said, 'Yes, it's true, what we have prayed for has occurred and to our humble family! Kisha has touched the immortals!'"

"Tears came to his eyes, Taya," Kisha added. "And to mine. What an experience! Oh, how can I thank you?"

"It wasn't just me, Kisha," Taya whispered. "You have the three young men to thank too."

"You haven't explained to me why they were so willing," Kisha said. "Did they know?"

"No, they knew nothing, and even if they knew, they wouldn't understand. They had to experience what they desired. How can one explain these things, Kisha, when their minds are elsewhere?"

"Yes, you're right," Kisha said. "We wouldn't want them to go mad. But I feel such sorrow in them."

"I know," Taya said. "We shall see. Desire forms deep roots but still there's hope."

After Kisha left, the young men told Taya that they had overheard his conversation. They begged him to explain.

He refused. What happened, he said, was a private matter of Kisha. Only Kisha can share such information.

"Yet we remember so little about the episode. Don't we deserve to know something?"

"You do know," Taya said. "There's no mystery. You were there."

"What do you mean? Yes we were there, but what happened?" they encircled him, their minds anxious for insight.

"Look at you!" Taya responded. "Filled with confusion and lack of fulfillment, unable now to face or understand what had happened. Even your skin shows a struggle with something. Now look at Kisha. She is more wondrous than ever. Try to recall."

"Just tell us," they pleaded as they followed him out, "did it ever happen? That's all we want to know. Was she there, was she with us, did we see her naked, did we touch her? What happened?"

The End

Our Sister Brophy

Our sister Brophy had two eyes, but they were each a different shape and size, and their colors changed with the season. It seemed that each eye had its own mission too, which was disconcerting when looking at or speaking with her. Brophy's mouth, some people believed, looked like a botched work of plastic surgery. It had a continuous smile and the upper lip never moved while the lower stretched almost to the cheek bones. Eyebrows and eyelashes did not exist on her face, and one of her ears had no outer part. Except for the top of her head, she had no hair, which also changed color and texture depending on the season. My mother tried to disguise it by dying and straightening her hair, but we weren't fooled.

Her appearance was nothing like ours and we always wondered if she was adopted. Every year, in an effort to convince us, my mother repeated the story of her long pregnancy and birth to answer every question or doubt. But her story did not seem even like an abnormal birth story; it resembled a fairy tale. After all, Brophy did look like someone from a fairy tale.

Brophy enjoyed and expanded upon my mother's strained explanation; she began to talk about herself as if she belonged in that fairy tale, as if she didn't know that fairy tale creatures, including princes and princesses, did not look like she did. One of them might temporarily turn into a frog or other animal, but soon enough, in the end, their human essence was revealed. But this fact did not seem to occur to her. Instead the stories seemed to comfort her. My brother and I feared she was drowning in a delusion. Out of concern for her mental stability, my brother gently told her,

"You're not a fairy tale character, or, if you are, soon you should be turning into something else. Some prince is not going to come along and kiss you and reveal who you truly are, and the evil witch who made you look this way won't shrivel up and die. There's no spell, Brophy."

Our attempts were without effect. Brophy liked the fairy tale explanation of her existence, or at least she did not reject it.

Part of the blame for this ongoing confusion must fall upon my mother and father.

"Yes, sweetie, that makes perfect sense," my mother would say to Brophy when she explored her fairy tale origins, "doesn't it, Ralph?"

Ralph, my father, would shake his head as if he wasn't completely assenting or dissenting, but, most importantly, not denying the truth of it.

"Mom," I would say in private, "stop agreeing with her. She's not the victim of some curse or spell. You made that up. We don't have witches and demons. She's what she is."

"How do we know?" my mother, in an innocent tone, would reply.

And my brother would say,

"Because we don't live in a fairy tale, Mom!"

"How do we know?" she would repeat. "Perhaps those writers of fairy tales were writing about something they'd actually seen in this world; perhaps we're living in a world that will at any time turn into something else, some better or worse version of what we have now. How can you be so sure of what reality this is?"

My brother and I would turn to my father, hoping that he would provide some rational counter-argument.

"Interesting," he would say, as if deep in thought. "Yes, quite interesting. Think about it for a moment. How do we truly know what layers are within this existence?"

"Brophy's not living in some layer," I corrected him. "She's right here with us. If she's in a fairy tale, then so are you and I and all of us."

"Exactly!" my head-in-the-clouds father would say.

Her teachers did not help. Brophy not only had an abnormal appearance, she also a mind that functioned differently. If I was a teacher, I would have gently escorted her out of the class long ago, but her questions and behavior fascinated the school staff.

In her math class, the teacher asked if anyone could explain a calculus problem.

Brophy stood up and said, almost as if she was the teacher,

"Before I do that, let's first try to understand addition. Can anyone explain how one plus one is always two? I know of many incidents where one plus one does not equal two."

She grabbed an apple from one place and an orange from another, and asked everyone:

"Does this apple and this orange equal two."

One of her peers said, "Yeah, because they together are two objects."

"So any object and any other object will always make two, regardless of size, regardless of time or dimension."

"Of course," the kid answered.

"But what is 'one'? What does 'one' mean? If these two objects can equal two without knowing what each 'one' is, then how can anyone know that they can equal two? Perhaps they equal four million ones."

"You're weird!" another student said.

Others laughed.

"If you can't understand the meaning of 'one'," Brophy scolded, "then you can't grasp the meaning of two. Where I come from…"

As soon as Brophy said, "where I come from...," the students led out sounds of frustration, such as, 'here we go again.'

"You come from here, Brophy," a student sitting next to her said. "You're like the rest of us. Sit down."

"No, you don't understand. I don't come from here, and I've never come from here."

"An alien?" a girl up front said.

"No, I'm not an alien, if you mean someone from another planet. Nope."

Then the teacher would step in and stop a train of events that she had seen too often in the past.

"Brophy can think anything she wishes about her origins. But she makes an interesting point. What is one?"

Brophy smiled and sat down, quite happy about her tiny victory. At lunch she would share the event with my brother and me, seemingly unaware that on each occasion she was distancing himself further from her peers.

There were other incidents.

In the middle of the night my brother found her in his bed, almost on top of him, pulling at something in the air.

My brother, startled and afraid he was being attacked, yelled, and my whole family came to his room.

"Brophy! What are you doing?" my father said.

We all stared at Brophy, wanting an explanation.

"I'm sorry," she said in a meek voice to my brother. "I thought you were having a nightmare and struggling against something."

"That's not true," my brother said. "You had your hands on my face and were moving my face around and touching my arms and neck. It was gross. Yuck! What's wrong with you?"

"Sorry, really I am," Brophy said and walked away, my parents following her into her room.

On another occasion, I woke up half-asleep pinned against my closet door by Brophy, and Brophy saying, out of breath,

"Stay there, don't move, I'll be right back."

I faintly recall seeing her appear to grab someone's hair and face and hold his or her head. I awoke the next morning in my bed and assumed it was just a dream and tried to forget about it.

On several nights my brother experienced similar incidents in which Brophy was on his bed, touching his face, arms, hands and legs, and fighting with something yet pushing on his face.

At the same time, in both of our bedrooms, Brophy would be rearranging pictures, lamps, desks, and other articles, as if she was molding the space.

My brother and I tried to convince ourselves that her behavior was harmless. Perhaps she was sleep walking. She never hurt us or attempted anything inappropriate. But the more we experienced the episodes, the more her actions seemed as if she was battling something.

Our mother as usual told us to ignore her, but in time that advice—typical of my mother if nothing troubling had occurred—no longer satisfied us. My brother and I decided to sit down and talk to Brophy in a different way.

After school in an empty classroom we started discussing her rants in class.

"You have to stop what you're doing," I explained to her in as kind a tone as I could manage, "or you won't have any friends."

"Already people think you're on the way to an asylum," my brother added.

"We're really worried," I said. "You talk about these things as if you believe them. And what are you doing at night? You know you were born in a hospital and our mother was your mother, right? You know this, right?"

"Mom says..." Brophy interjected.

"Forget what Mom says," I said, "forget it. She's trying to help you cope. You're different, we understand, but Mom won't let that be. She's desperate to explain why you're different, as if she knows. But she doesn't. No one knows."

"I do," Brophy said. "I've always known. I've known before my birth."

"Stop it, Brophy, stop it," my brother said impatiently. "You know no such thing. Look, you don't have to explain how or why you exist. No one does. You exist, that's it."

"He's right," I added. "You can be different. You don't have to explain. Just live your life and accept yourself."

"If I did something miraculous right now, would you believe me?" Brophy asked.

We shook our heads.

"Miracles don't make you different or special," I said. "Miracles happen all of the time. Who cares?"

"Suppose I disappeared, right before your eyes? Would you then admit that Brophy's not one of us?"

Again we shook our head.

"Where was I the first six years of my life?" Brophy asked.

My brother and I looked at each other and responded with what our mother told us:

"You were in a special hospital because of your body. The doctors were examining you, trying to help you, giving you surgery."

"Do you believe that?" Brophy asked.

In fact, we had never believed it. We thought our parents found, adopted, or were forced to take Brophy. We never liked her explanation of the first years of Brophy's life.

Brophy noticed our hesitation.

"Of course you don't believe it," Brophy said. "Bless her heart, mother created a story about my early years. And why don't you believe it? Because you can't imagine that your mother gave birth to this, this deformed creature, me. You wouldn't believe I was your sister and you definitely wouldn't believe I'm your protector."

"What did you say?" my brother said, standing up in surprise. "Protector?"

"It's true."

"And what has your appearance to do with being a protector?" I asked. "Why does a protector need no eyelashes or eyebrows and have hair that changes every season? What does that have to do with it?"

Brophy did not reply. She remained quiet, as if she was trying to think what to say.

Eventually her silence began to bother us. Perhaps we had gone too far. Breaking her view of her existence could destroy how she saw her world and make her depressed.

"I'm sorry," she apologized. "I thought you were old enough. You live in such a limited realm. I don't know how to explain it."

"What realm?" my brother asked, again not believing her. "What do you see?"

"I don't 'see'," she replied. "I 'live' in another realm. And creatures from that realm want to harm people in this realm. And they know I can travel to it and that you are the people I exist with. They seek ways to enter this realm, your realm. And their means and their actions you would find terrifying."

My brother and I quickly glanced at each other, both wondering if we should continue to play along with this new and far more outrageous continuation of our mother's already ridiculous explanation.

"Why don't they like our realm?" I asked in a skeptical tone.

"Perfection," Brophy said.

"Uh-huh," my brother said. "Perfection. You mean everything..."

"And everyone," Brophy added. "Their realm is perfect. Nothing is out of place. Nothing is mistaken. No one has flaws. Nothing is imperfect or unbalanced. It's like Plato's Forms. They have what people in your realm seek, their objects are the perfect objects, they are the models, their tears are the perfect tears—"

"—and one plus one...?" I asked, remembering her math lecture.

"One plus one does equal two because each one there is perfect and can make a perfect two, because what is between one and the plus and the other one is perfectly symmetrical, whereas here we never have a perfect one or a perfect plus."

"So you're protecting us from perfection?" my brother said, trying to hold back a smile, if not a laugh.

"Mock if you wish, but nothing is more frightening than the power and standards of perfection."

"Are there others like you," I asked, "protectors, or those who can straddle two realms?"

"Perhaps, but I've never met any. Those from the perfect realm can only survive here very briefly and they must return. I'm a freak, both here and there. Imperfection for them is not only contagious but destructive of mental stability."

"So you're alone in this, as far as you know?" my brother asked. "No one else knows about your mission and the problems of imperfection?"

"Mom knows."

"Really?" I asked. "How long has she known?"

"From the beginning."

"And where and when was your beginning?" my brother wondered.

"Every year," she said. "I begin every year. I'm born every year with the age and time I choose."

My brother could no longer hold back how he felt and burst into laughter.

"Oh Brophy," he said, "you really need to get some help. You're just someone who was born with birth defects. It happens to a lot of people."

When he said this, I was thinking: 'If our mother didn't give birth to Brophy, and if Brophy didn't endure six years of rehabilitation and surgery, as our mother told us but which my brother and I never believed, then why does Brophy look so disordered? Her entire body always is and was out of proportion. Her mind, however, was quite balanced and stable.

"So every year," I repeated, "the process of entering this realm distorts your features? Yet every year you enter with the same features? Or is your face and features considered perfect in your realm?"

"Of course not," Brophy said. "I'm a monster when I first return to that perfect realm. I must fix myself. When I return here, I try to repeat the distortions of imperfection because that's how I'm known here. Yet making imperfection is very difficult to repeat for those in our realm, as you can see from my face, but fortunately no one here is bothered by my errors and changes. You all are accustomed to imperfection. It doesn't drive you mad. I try each year to correct the errors, but the process became worse. That's the strange feature of imperfect beings. They're imperfect, but their imperfection is closer to perfection than to complete imperfection. I haven't yet been able to master such imperfection."

"So each year you have experienced birth and imperfection in this realm," my brother repeated.

"Yes, and then I return to my own realm of perfection for renewal, and after renewal I return to guard you, my family, from the threats of those in the realm of perfection."

"And who is your family in the realm of perfection?" I asked.

"I have no family," she answered, "None of us do. Family is imperfect there. Here I love family. It's so beautifully imperfect."

"When did you meet our mother?"

"I met her when she was six. I became her imaginary friend. I promised her I would protect her family in the future if she would do one favor for me. I was young and she was young and we both had no grasp of the consequences of this favor."

"The favor?" I asked.

"I wanted to bring back from the imperfect realm someone imperfect and show her off to my teacher. I never realized how dangerous and complicated that process could be. She aged several years. I decided I would do more than protect her family when the time came, I would somehow return those years to her."

"How could you do that?" my brother asked.

"By diminishing my own life," Brophy said. "But my sacrifice had an unforeseen effect, almost like a miracle. By making myself imperfect and still of the same substance as those in the perfect world, I found I could remain far longer in your realm than anyone I knew in the perfect realm. Being able to remain in your realm, I was able to keep away those who entered and who tried to force perfection, often violently, on your people."

"So you protect more than my brother and me," I said.

"Yes, if I can, but I can't be everywhere."

"When will you give our mother her years back?" my brother asked.

"Oh, I did that years ago," Brophy said, smiling. "Your mother never knew."

"These things you do," my brother said, "they seem far beyond the small favor my mother did."

"Small favor?" Brophy said, almost harshly. "Hardly. She risked her life to enter the realm of perfection."

"How often have we been in danger?" I asked.

"Several hundred times, but they couldn't succeed because I battled them and because they couldn't remain long enough to succeed. For that reason, your mother tried to make it appear I was adopted, so that I would have a legitimate reason to be near the two of you. You see, they come, and they try to make changes to you and your brother to create perfection, because they don't appreciate or understand imperfection. They fear it. They don't see how it gives each entity of existence, including you, a character. They don't see the art. In my realm, there's no art because art is perfectly imperfect. It can always be improved."

We were so astonished that we could not speak. One fact was true: they flowed from her mind as if she was speaking honestly. She did not hesitate or contemplate how she would continue this story.

"And that is why I look the way I do," Brophy added. "I've tried to approximate your imperfection, but on each occasion I've failed. I'm not an artist. I wish I was. Finally, I did what you all do. I've learned to be content with my imperfections here, however ugly and atrocious to my realm they may seem. Originally, I thought I was being creative with imperfection, you know, taking away the ear flesh, eliminating the eyebrows, and so on, but obviously, I'm not an artist. And it's art. You've so many wonderfully imperfect beings.

"But they don't understand. They come and try to make perfection by influencing the minds of your leaders or artists or thinkers or anyone to "improve" your systems and processes. I stop them. That's what I've been doing. And I'm glad now you know. Your mother has worried about you thinking badly of me. Now she can relax."

My brother sat with his mouth open, realizing the number of incidents in our lives that now made more sense, even if she had fabricated everything.

"I apologize," Brophy said, standing up, "I realize that an attempt at perfection is happening now and I must go. Forgive me for not telling you sooner. I love you, my brother and sister."

We waved good-bye to her, looked at each other in disbelief, and had only one thought. How fortunate we were to have such a sister protecting imperfection.

THE END

The Ice People

During weeks of frigid air and snow in Toronto, the wind chill eventually reached forty below centigrade. Icicles hung from the wires above the streets; and the sides of buildings began to change color as the frost was entombing the structures. Stranded cars littered the streets. Fire engines and ambulances constantly responded to inadequate wiring, heating and plumbing. City workers, outside all day trying to keep up with too many problems, labored with stiff red faces, puffy yellow uniforms and high boots, their eyes barely visible behind the face protectors. The weather doomed them with the worst jobs that month. As if anyone needed the reminder, every ten minutes radio weather announcers were scaring residents with their chant that thirty-five below could freeze human flesh and "Stay home!" People were staying home. Who would want to leave their homes? The sidewalks were barren; the stores empty, and the skating rinks had only the ghosts of past skaters.

Beyond these unfortunate situations, the homeless were in far more dire circumstances. City rescue workers, religious groups, and other organizations searched for those who could not go home, whose homes were on the streets, and too often they found a frozen man or woman. There were simply not enough places because more than the homeless were without heat. The churches, temples, mosques, community centers, and other institutional spaces were jammed with people not usually homeless, and the city could not open up two vacant armories due to liability problems. Even if the city did, many veteran street people would have refused to sleep next to strangers six inches apart in giant cavern-like rooms where the lights never went out and they feared to lose their few possessions and dogs. No, they would prefer the vents and entrances from subways. Even after the evening sweep, the spots near the subway vents quickly filled up again with other bundled up bodies sucking up the little streams of warmth through the large grates. Many of them had no mittens or head coverings, their faces and eyes showing the expression of panic and the stares of acceptance, especially when nearby was the entrance to THE PATH, the world's largest underground shopping mall that ran beneath almost the entire downtown Toronto core. Down there during the day, in a space that could potentially hold thousands of homeless, where the air was warm and cozy, walked busy employed people who already had homes and wanted security and freedom from the beggars on the street.

In this time of terrible need for the homeless, one group, led by Ankala Imfredo, put into action a plan after years of frustration. When he first arrived as an immigrant, after his activist party had failed to drive the dictator and his party out of power, after they had wiped out the people in his village, he lived through his first winter and witnessed the disparity of THE PATH and the shocking number of homeless on the cold winter nights. In his village in the old country, people always had at least a home, even if with a neighbor, even if other necessities, such as food, water and medical attention, were not as available or tainted. If they were without a home or food, his family and others tried to help them. In Toronto, these poor discarded folks had none of these necessities without begging and hoping. By the next winter, Ankala started an organization and activist group to try to resolve the problem. After a few years with little response from the government, he realized a more radical solution might be needed.

A large ice block encasing an upright man, his eyes open, with a nametag hung around his neck, was set down in front of old City Hall, greeting business people, casual walkers, shoppers, and most significantly, government workers on their way to work. The tag read: "Help the Homeless."

While the government was trying to determine the identity of the one encased in ice, two mornings later Ankala arranged to have displayed another fully dressed person in an ice block at the harbor, near the harbor police building. Around her neck was the same message: "Help the Homeless."

As Ankala expected, the media and the general public initially assumed that someone had recently killed the people by imprisoning them in ice. Upon a more thorough examination of the bodies, authorities learned the truth: the ice people died naturally first and then someone froze them in the ice block. Though the media published their faces everywhere, no one came forth to identify the bodies.

The next week passersby found a third person encased in ice beside the Toronto Star newspaper headquarters, not too far from the second person in ice. The third note was exactly the same as the others: "Help the Homeless."

Ankala hoped that the difficulties raised by the ice people would become a problem for all levels of government and the police, but the officials pondered more how than why the ice people appeared. The primary headaches were that no person or group had claimed responsibility for the attacks.

Another week passed without incident in Toronto, but similar events Ankala had arranged in New York and London, though the bodies were not in ice but on park benches in Hyde Park and Central Park wrapped in plastic wrap, again with the tag, "Help the Homeless."

American and British authorities conferred with Canadian officials on a plan of action. The crisis was baffling. In New York and London, the corpses also had natural deaths before they were wrapped; and again no one came to identify them. Their fingerprints brought no identification.

The snow continued without mercy in Toronto, the temperature remained colder than usual, and the wind blasted its way in defiance up and down the major streets. The icicles on some buildings reached several stories in length. Massive drifts had climbed up the downtown buildings or blocked the streets so that every night the city turned into a desolate area that the homeless had almost to themselves, creatively using the snow and ice to build shelters and wind shields.

At the end of January, as if to conclude a month of disaster with an exclamation point, the power failed in a large group of buildings in the downtown core and Ankala's group brazenly took advantage of a strained police and government coping with the weather and the drain on the grid by briefly abducting the Mayor. The kidnappers had one demand: Solve the homeless problem. In twenty-four hours, they released the mayor. To Ankala the abduction of the mayor was only a threat of what his group could do, if they chose. He never intended to ransom or harm the mayor.

At the same time, the fourth person in a block of ice appeared in front of a mansion in Rosedale, a wealthy upscale neighborhood. "Help the Homeless" appeared again.

The police brought each of the leaders of the homeless organizations to private meetings. They interrogated each of them about the ice people.

"I know nothing about the ice people," Ankala told the agents.

"If you're innocent, then you won't mind helping us stop the people who are doing this," they said.

"No, I can't," Ankala said, "not unless concrete steps are taken to solve the homeless problem and quickly.

"It's your choice," the agents said. "Would you prefer to spend your time in jail as a suspect or to work covertly with us to find the perpetrators of these ice people?"

"It would be dishonorable," he replied, "if I didn't ask for something in return for the promise to end appearances of the ice people. And if I had no honor, I might as well be in jail."

"Or," they added, "we could ship you back to your old country."

"As you wish," Ankala replied, "I have no interest in betraying those who respect me. These people only want something done. They don't intend to hurt anyone. After all, they released the mayor."

There was an hour of stalemate while the officials conferred.

The agents surprised Ankala by complying with his terms and said that they would begin new policies and approaches to diminish the problem.

"In light of these assurances, will you help us?" they asked.

"No," Ankala responded again, and then he added, "I have no interest in your plans or your words. I want action. I want steps being taken. I want money poured into helping the homeless. I want money taken from less urgent projects and placed in helping the homeless. Then, if you do this and I see action, I agree."

It was a courageous but not a diplomatic answer. Ankala found it difficult to trust government. In his native land, he had seen government betray many promises; he had watched the government steal private property and farms and drag their owners in the middle of the night and shoot them; he had witnessed the military come and kill everyone in his village and destroy their homes and crops.

His refusal to accept their terms was not stubbornness. Years ago, when he first started his plan to help the homeless, Ankala was determined never to back down in his purpose. He had heard the politicians' promises for years. If he gave his approval to a plan that might never happen, without concrete action, then all the attempts to assist the homeless—the years of going door to door to find spaces, the ice people, and the abduction of the mayor—would have been wasted. He also knew that it would require many months of behind-the-scenes work at all levels of government before a solution would happen. He had to see action, not promises.

In the next week, the government of Canada decided to deport Ankala Imfredo to his native country for lying on his immigration papers and in his interview. He had not told the authorities in his application that he was involved in a group that opposed the government in his native country. No one challenged this reason because it was true. Ankala did conceal his anti-government activities and his native land had no reason to protest the ruling. They were glad to see him move to Canada so that he and his group were out of the country.

After the news of Ankala's deportation, no ice people appeared, but hundreds of cardboard life-size figures of Ankala himself did surface one morning in London, Toronto, and New York in honor of him; and, as if to grant a small wish that had come too late, the weather suddenly became mild and no more homeless died from exposure.

In his native land, Ankala was tried, found guilty, and executed for anti-government activities. Before he was executed, he dropped to his knees, grabbed a handful of dirt, and brought it to his nose to smell. Then he raised the hand of soil up to the sun and gave thanks in his heart for the wonder of nature and his chance to experience its many joys when he was a farmer in his homeland. As they executed him, his face had a smile from the expectation he would see in the afterlife those friends and family slaughtered in his village, their deaths the reason he became a rebel and finally left his native land.

After his death, in the customary end for traitors, the government left his corpse to rot in a death pit exposed to the sun to be picked away by wildlife.

No creature or sun had the opportunity. Ankala had left instructions to his fellow activists to bribe the guards and bury his body properly in the soil of his home village. They happily complied with his request, but they went further in his honor.

In the following winter, the underground crowd on THE PATH could not miss a sealed clear plastic case containing a life size carved wooden mahogany statue of Ankala Imfredo, a man without home or country, who fought for those who could not fight in his native home, and for those without homes in his adopted land.

THE END

The Bird

Not long after the death of Mistress Marasa, the most successful card reader in the region, her son Charles took up her work. Charles, a blond, thin, tall man with a goatee, was trained as a pianist, but he had always wanted to follow in his mother's footsteps, even though she had always discouraged him, pointing out the "dangers" of advising people on their futures.

Two months after his mother died, a bird appeared on a branch very close to the large diamond shaped stained-glass window that faced the street. At the time, Charles was playing the piano in the corner of his studio and listening to the bird singing very loudly. It was a dark blue bird with purple wing tips, purple belly, and orange ringed eyes perched on a branch.

From then on, the bird came every day and perched on the sill or a nearby branch, the bird and he peering into each other's eyes, only the glass separating them. Charles could not identify the type, but he knew it was the same kind of bird, perhaps the same bird. It stayed for hours before it flew away each day. While watching him it would sing its own musical phrases along with the piano, its music having a strange ineffable effect on him, as if the bird was trying to communicate.

Since he was alone most of the time, Charles initially appreciated the visits of the bird. It was almost like a pet. But when the harsh weather arrived, its continuing presence puzzled and worried him. With only the front tree as protection, and the building breaking the wind from only one direction, its survival seemed unlikely; but each day it appeared, in freezing snow, burning sun, or violent rainstorms, regardless of weather. He hoped, for its own protection, it would seek shelter; but it stubbornly remained.

Charles' clients spread the news about the bird. Birders checked on its origins and found that the bird was not indigenous to their area. They too were perplexed. How could an exotic bird, through many shifts in weather, survive outside of his window and sit there and stare day upon day?

Rumors about the "creature" that no weather condition could affect began to circulate. More and more people came to stare at it. One client told Charles that the bird was mocking her for coming to him. A few customers were afraid to leave his studio after the bird's stares, afraid the bird would attack them once outside and follow them home.

Other fortune tellers were losing business from the attention to Charles' bird and began to spread the idea that it was not a bird but a demon or a supernatural creature. Anyone, they warned, should fear going anywhere near the bird.

Mistress Shahira, once a fierce rival of Charles' mother, said the bird was Charles's reincarnated mother, Mistress Marasa. Marasa had returned as a bird to exact vengeance on those who had not used her services or followed her advice.

*

When Jessica, once a client of Mistress Marasa, visited Charles, she moved her chair beside the window to look at the bird more closely.

"Could I have it?" Jessica asked after a minute of examination.

"Could you have it?" Charles said with a smile. "It's not a toy or something I can sell or give. It's wild. If it wants to be with you, it'll be with you. I have no chains on it."

"If you say yes, I'll net or trap it somehow. I'd like it for my collection."

He hesitated and looked at the bird. The intense stare of the bird could be eerie sometimes, but he enjoyed its company and its song when playing the piano. He only fretted about its survival.

"Please!" she pestered. "Can't I take it? I have a giant cage in my back yard. I would love to have that bird. It's so beautiful. In the winter I bring them all into a large two-story heated garage. It will live longer, don't worry."

"I'm not stopping it from leaving," Charles said. "If it wants to go to your cage, it will."

As he said these words, he realized that perhaps Jessica's cage would help it survive in this climate. After all, how long could it endure? When does it eat? His birdseed certainly was not enough.

"That bird should already be dead and it's not," Jessica said. "People say it's Mistress Marasa haunting you, trying to stop you. A spirit might do that, try to make sure you fail. If she's in a cage with other birds, she won't haunt anyone. If you let it stay, you're going to lose business. People might take offense. You know, don't you, that we all feared going to your mother? She was strange and we never knew what she would say. But we were compelled."

"Why should anyone take offense?" Charles asked. "The bird bothers no one. And it's not my mother."

"How do you know?" Jessica wondered, as she prepared to leave. "How do you know who it is and who it's haunting? Perhaps it harasses your customers when they leave, keeps track of them, and visits them in their sleep. You, a fortune teller, should know better. Your mother had powers."

After Jessica left, another customer, sweating heavily and shaking, his eyes looking as if he was on fire inside, cautiously sat down, moving his head around as if he sensed someone else was in the room.

"Where's the bird?" he asked nervously. "Where is it? Where? Where?"

When Charles pointed at the window, the man gasped and screamed, then ran out the door.

He returned in a few moments and sat down again; but asked for the bird to tell his fortune. Charles' mother had told his fortune and promised him she would come back from the grave to assure him. He needed her.

"Tell the bird to talk," he ordered Charles. "Tell it, tell it!"

Charles explained he had no influence on the bird, that it was only a bird.

The man departed almost in tears.

An old heavyset woman visited and laughed when she saw the bird. She was draped more than dressed in a bright, multi-colored frock from neck to toe. On her head was more a headpiece than a hat, and more than enough space for the bird to nest. Her face was caked with make-up, the heavy eyeliner circles and deep blue eye shadow especially noticeable.

"So that's the bird," she said with a Romanian accent. "Yes, well, it could be your mother. Everyone says it's your mother. Your mother spoke to me about the afterlife. Does it help you?"

"What?" Charles said. "Help?"

"Help you make decisions. You need help, don't you? You're not your mother, you know? Does it help you?"

"No, the bird doesn't help me."

"Oh, that's too bad. Your mother didn't want you to be like her, you know."

"I know," Charles said.

"She didn't want you to go through what she did. But they tortured her at the end."

"What? What are you talking about? You knew her?"

"Of course I knew her. We all knew her. She was the most gifted reader of us all, and I know all who have real gifts. I'm Mistress Angela from Romania. Mistress Shahira, one of my protégés, asked me to come and observe the bird and see what it is. Your mother told me before she died that they were coming for her. She knew, she knew."

"Who? Who was coming?" Charles asked impatiently. "I don't recall seeing you."

"Oh, you were never here when I came. I don't know where you were. But, mark my words, you don't want to end that way. If, that is, you have her gifts. They know."

"Who knows? What are you talking about? My mother died peacefully in her sleep. I was there."

"It may have seemed peaceful to the eye," Mistress Angela said, "but in truth it wasn't peaceful. None of us in this profession enter the beyond peacefully. The very gifted pay even more for the privilege. There's judgement and there are monitors to insure the payment is made. But don't worry. It's done. Her suffering is over."

Then she suddenly changed the subject.

"Does the bird give a sign or a sound to tell you about certain cards?"

"The bird has nothing to do with the cards," Charles repeated what he had said to others. "It appeared not long after I started doing the reading, and has come and gone ever since, though I worry for it in harsh weather. I kind of like it, it's a beautiful bird, and its sings beautifully too, but I admit it frightens some people."

"Well yes, of course it does, understandably. The darn thing terrifies me. I hope they never send me a wild one. Best to get one in a cage, not a wild one like that. Perhaps a caged bird will ward it off."

"What do you mean? Who 'sends a wild one'?"

"They do, those from the beyond. In another life, when I was a man in Africa, I foretold some frightening things. In time, a vulture came to an area that had never seen a vulture. And the vulture did its work."

"What did it do?"

"The details are erased from my mind. It was another life. All I recall was that I received punishment. Your bird too has a role to play. All birds are dinosaurs, primeval creatures, millions of years old, almost before time. Seeded in their little brains is the answer to many questions. The bird carries messages throughout time. That bird is sent for a reason.

"So!" the old woman changed the subject again and returned to the card reading. "I have come for one purpose. Please allow me to give you a reading."

Out of professional courtesy, Charles nodded. They went to the table.

"Let's see what they say about you," she said. "Let's see what gifts you have."

*

Another visitor came later that evening and glared at the bird.

"Do you know me?" she asked.

"No, I'm sorry," Charles said. "Should I?"

"I suppose not. You're new. I'm Mistress Shahira."

Whereas Charles wore a clean white shirt and dark pants, like someone ready to bag groceries at the food store, Mistress Shahira appeared in stature and dress like a great noblewoman of old Europe, prepared for a ball and the next dance with the prince.

"Your mother and I knew each other for many years but, well," Shahira spoke very slowly as if her every word was a royal decree, "we weren't on friendly terms and frankly I think she was jealous. It happens. Anyway, that's neither here nor there. I've heard about your bird. And there it is."

"It's not my bird," Charles said. "It's free to go wherever it wants."

"But it doesn't, does it? That's the mystery. It only goes here, as far as we know. A wild bird who returns to this one location. I find that curious, very curious. Don't you?"

"Of course I do. But animals have ways we'll never understand. We can barely understand humans."

"So true, so true. But birds aren't people. Some of them do the bidding of the beyond."

"I don't know about that."

"You don't know about the beyond?" she asked.

"I don't know that this bird is doing the bidding of the beyond."

"Didn't your mother talk about the beyond? No? I guess she wouldn't. She didn't want to involve you in her work. But certain wild birds are servants of the beyond and visit those living earthly lives."

"What can I do for you?" Charles asked. He didn't want to hear anything more about the bird or the beyond. "Would you like a reading?"

"I?" Shahira exclaimed in surprise. "From you? Heavens no. I get my readings from my mentor, Mistress Angela, whom I believe you've met. But I'd like you to invite you to my place for a reading. Free of charge."

Charles could not understand why she, or Mistress Angela for that matter, would want to tell his fortune and looked at her quizzically.

"Yes, I know," she answered. "You wonder why this person before you would want to give you a reading, don't you? It's quite simple. The bird. The bird has fascinated us all. I need to see what the cards say about you and the bird. What does this bird mean?"

"Don't bother," Charles immediately reacted. "I'll tell you what your mentor said."

"I don't want to know!" Shahira interrupted. "And, by the way, never tell anyone what another fortune teller has said in private. Never!"

"Fine, but it's hardly different from what you'd expect. It's exactly what my mother said. The reading doesn't bother me. What bothers me is that someone has told people that the bird's my mother. Others say it's a demon and prefer to talk about it rather than their future, and the rest want to know how it applies to their future."

"Ah! You see?" Shahira said. "The point I raise. Many interesting facets. Come tomorrow night. I've invited several others to witness your reading. They want to meet the man with the bird."

"I'll think about it," Charles said.

She leaned down next to his face.

"Let's hope the bird comes too," she whispered in his ear.

*

From his own curiosity about his rivals Charles went to the gathering at Shahira's house. Though Charles had never met any of them when his mother was alive—she kept him away from anything concerning card reading—his mother did talk about Shahira, Angela, and other card readers, and he wanted to see them in person.

The contrast in life-style was immediately apparent. Charles' place of work reflected his dress. He did his reading in a room—the same room his mother had used—that doubled as a living room, dining room, and kitchen. A spiral staircase led to an upstairs with two small bedrooms and a bathroom. The Spartan appearance was intentional. Though his mother was very successful and left him quite a sum of money when she passed, she did not believe in show or intimidating her customers. Her wealthy clients were treated no better than the janitor who lived in the attic apartment down the street.

Shahira's place of business was like a small palace compared to his own abode. The marble floors, original paintings and sculpture, tall ceilings, and furniture that was merely for show, reminded him more of a museum or art gallery. She even had a place to train fortune tellers.

He noticed a caged bird too.

Shahira saw him looking at it.

"Yes, I have my own bird now," Shahira sighed. "It's tame, of course. I'm recommending a bird to all my colleagues. A caged bird keeps away the wild bird and gives a certain—how can I say?—primal power to the atmosphere, don't you think? And it brings in business too, as I've told all these ladies. Clients feel safer here than in your home where the wild bird perches and could attack them. Of course, your bird is, well, unique because it's probably your mother. To have your mother visit you as a wild bird, my, my, my, that's something. But who knows? If not your mother, what is it?"

Charles quickly saw that Mistress Shahira was the star to her fellow fortune tellers, often because she bribed them with clients she did not want or need. This parasitical relationship with other fortune tellers angered his mother, who saw the relationship of client and reader as almost sacred. A card reader, she said, shouldn't "sell off" her clients for money or influence, as if the relationship meant nothing.

Mistress Shahira, hoping at some point the bird might appear, encouraged Charles to talk about the bird to the group. Charles had little to say except what he had already told Shahira and Angela. Whether the bird had some mystical significance was a question he could not answer. Best to leave such matters alone. His mother had long ago impressed on him the ramifications of becoming a card reader. She said:

"Charlie, if it's not dangerous, it's not real. To see into the unknown is like walking into a dark cave. You never know if you'll be bitten, find gold, or be buried forever. Every day I walk into that cave. The frauds? They deceive the desperate and never face danger; they never tempt the unknown."

The bird never appeared at Mistress Shahira's home. Her toadies all went home disappointed, though Charles was pleased that the bird would not come to this opulent home or be among this group. His mother would have smiled.

"I'm sure my bird scared it away," Mistress Shahira explained. "And, in a way, I'm glad. Thank goodness the creatures from beyond aren't yet interested in me."

*

When he returned home, the bird was not at the window, but in the morning, it came back and sat on the sill focused as always on Charles.

For a long time, Charles had wondered if the bird would enter if he opened the window. When it was away, he would leave mounds of seeds on the sill, but he had never opened the window when it was present. The idea frightened him because of the warning of others. Would the bird attack him? Would it refuse to leave once it was inside? After all, it was wild.

He decided to take the risk. He opened the window and the bird flew into the room and landed upon the piano, staring directly at Charles. The window remained open so the bird could leave whenever it wanted. Even the piano sound did not disturb it. It remained fixed and started to sing.

At the same time one of Mistress Angela's spies noticed that the bird had flown into the room. The watchdog alerted Mistress Angela and she arrived soon after.

The bird began to screech at her.

"If you've come to gawk at the bird, please leave," Charles said.

"I'm not here to gawk," she said, walking to the window and closing it, thereby trapping the bird within Charles' studio. "I'm here to take the bird and save you and others from danger."

Jessica walked in with a large net and cage to hold the bird.

Behind her were a couple of other people on the stairs that led up to his apartment. Outside on the street and sidewalk was a large crowd of people.

The bird continued to make sounds that were unlike any bird he had ever heard. They reminded him more of a large animal.

"I'm sorry," Jessica said, "really I am, but that bird remains a threat to all of us. If it's your mother, she's come to haunt us. That's not good. You have no idea how much she knew about us. I and others told her every secret. In the end, we were afraid of her. If it's not your mother but a messenger from the beyond, then we're all in danger, including you. Whatever it is, it's too weird. It's a threat. There's no way this bird is an ordinary bird. It must have a mission."

"In other words, this bird is not a bird at all," Mistress Angela concluded with confidence. "We know that. It's a spirit, perhaps good; but I think most likely bad, maybe the spirit of your mother, but certainly an unearthly being sent here to exact punishment or curse. I would worry, Charles. Mistress Shahira has begged me again to intervene and stop the terror this bird has brought."

"Get the bird, Jessica!" Mistress Angela ordered.

Jessica netted the bird as it was sitting on the piano in her net.

"Intervene again?" Charles asked. "Why did you intervene before?"

"Charles, those of us who seriously practice this profession walk continuously on dangerous ground. Your mother knew that, and so should you. We're dealing with the future, with other lives, their destinies. By telling people their future, we can change the future because people will often act on what we say and may decide to try to change their future. Do you think the forces of the universe want anyone to intervene in the future? No, they don't, unless...unless we ourselves are doing the wishes of the universe. Your mother knew that. She was very gifted and thus a threat not only to her clients and to herself, but to the way of things, to the beyond, even you. And not only she. We're all constantly under threat. We all must ponder if we dare disturb the universe.

"Come, Jessica. Bring the bird."

They began to leave, but Charles moved in front of them, wanting to know more.

"Your mother made a mistake," Mistress Angela complied in a sympathetic tone. "It happens. In this business it's easy enough to do and it affects all of us. She lied about a destiny, because she didn't want this person to know. When you lie, you make it seem the universe lies. The frauds do it all the time, but their lies are meaningless because they don't have the gift and can't read the future and they simply give to the clients what they want. The universe laughs at them. But when the gifted do it, well, the consequences are quite severe. Your mother knew. You see, it's bad enough to know and tell the future, but to tell a lie about the future when you know the future, that's like spitting in the face of the universe."

"What lie? What mistake? My mother was the most honest person I've ever known."

"To all but one. She was dishonest about the future of one person."

"Who?" Charles asked, becoming irritated by not knowing the name.

"You."

"What? Me?"

"Yes you," Mistress Angela explained. "She knew that the cards clearly said you'd be a card reader, like her. She knew it. And now I know it, because I too read the cards about you. No matter how she tried to deny it, she saw it. And I saw it. But never did she tell you or even hint what was the truth. In fact, she lied to you and tried to prevent you from becoming a fortune teller. She lied not once, but many times, from the time you were a boy. Can you deny it?"

No, he couldn't deny it. Charles recalled many conversations he had had with his mother about her work. He could also remember her reading his destiny. As a boy, he was in awe of what she did. Seeing all of the people asking her for help impressed him and he did think of copying his mother. But whenever he told her, whenever he admired her work, she diminished it, even mocking others in the profession, and encouraging him toward music and away from the cards. If he disagreed with her, she would become agitated and outline the dangers of the work to frighten him.

"This bird has some connection to all this, I'm sure," Mistress Angela continued. "I learned this from Mistress Shahira. Your mother told her in confidence that she would never allow her boy to become a card reader, even if it was his destiny. Perhaps, and I mean perhaps, if she had kept that one lie to herself, I wouldn't have confronted her and she may have lived longer and suffered less pain. Who knows? Her end would have been the same—the beyond makes no exceptions—but she would have lived a longer life. But Mistress Shahira and her neighbors had had enough of her acclaim and the way people feared her.

"So Shahira asked me to confront your mother, to warn her. When I did, she raged at me and told me that she didn't care, she wanted to protect her son, and so on. She made the lie public, she screamed it to the universe. The others had been patient too long with her. They too confronted her. On the night of her death, the night you said seemed peaceful, they came, and it wasn't peaceful. You weren't there then. You saw her afterward, when she was weak and the damage was done. But first she suffered greatly, so greatly that she was physically unable to withstand the pressure and she died. Gifts have consequences if misused. The universe demands obedience to its rules."

"Now we have the bird," Jessica in relief said, "and can end this."

"End what?" Charles said. "If it's an otherworldly bird, won't the beyond send another?"

"No," Mistress Angela said. "This bird is special, you'll see."

She began to walk down the steps, Jessica in front of her with the cage.

"And you can fulfill your destiny in peace, Charles. Your mother will no longer be able to keep you from it."

They showed the cage to the crowd outside. When the crowd saw it, they clapped and hollered, and trailed behind Jessica and Angela down the street toward Jessica's home. It was an odd procession, seeming almost like a sacred march toward holy grounds or the guillotine.

Charles was not pleased to see the bird go. He could have stopped Jessica from netting the bird, but he relented when he thought the bird would probably live longer in Jessica's cage.

He went to the piano and began to play one of his favorite Messiaen birdsong pieces.

As he was playing, another bird appeared at his window. He fell back off his piano stool when he saw it. He gathered himself and went to the window.

"Charles," the bird seemed to be saying in long drawn-out tones, though it could have been his own inner voice expressing doubts, "they're going to torture the bird. Save the bird."

Charles rushed out of his studio and ran down the street to the house of Jessica. A great mass of people, much larger than the one that had stood outside his window, surrounded the caged bird on the front lawn of her house. Underneath the cage were a pile of sticks and larger pieces of wood. Jessica and Angela lit a fire underneath and around the pile. The people were cheering them on while the bird was screeching as it had done previously, the fire started to rage around the cage.

Charles snatched the cage, raced back down the street to his studio, locked his door, and called the police. The people followed and shouted in anger to give them the bird. They threw rocks at his door and at the stain glass window and broke the window, but they could not reach his studio.

Finally the police came and the crowd dispersed.

When the evening had passed and the moon was full in the sky, Charles opened the cage and the bird flew away for a time, but soon it returned and perched in its usual spot at the window or flew into his apartment and sat on the piano.

*

Despite efforts of his rivals, Charles retained many of his mother's clients. People came from many regions and countries to witness the bird and at the same time to receive a reading. The bird in the end did not deter but attracted new customers. Charles suspected that the true purpose of the other fortune tellers had nothing to do with the lie. They wanted to drive his mother out of business because she was more gifted.

Even after Charles had passed away and someone else lived in the apartment, the bird continued its visits. Visitors also continued to monitor outside, waiting for the bird not to return or to die. After all, the bird had exceeded the life span of any bird. The media reported on it. Views of the bird had changed. Now they all pitied it, especially in increment weather, and realized that the bird was not a danger. They recalled what Charles had told them before he died: the bird daily reminded him of the dangers of entering the dark cave of the beyond and of other fortune tellers who might try to drive him away through envy. The bird was his protector.

Three months after Charles' death, in the middle of the night, another bird flew down and perched beside the first. When that happened, the two flew away into the night and the bird was never seen again.

THE END

Locals Only

Trevor walked into Trinity Bellwoods Park on a warm summer morning. The sky was a rich blue and the air was fresh with the smell of lilacs and the busy sounds of birds. Despite the heat, he wore a spring coat over a T-shirt, a wide-brimmed hat, and a pair of jeans with a kerchief around his neck.

The park was filled with children on the swings and playing in the sandboxes. Couples threw Frisbees. Runners in conversation passed Trevor on the track that circled the park.

Trevor turned his heavily scarred face away.

Off in the corner away from the main park but facing a gully below was the favorite bench where Trevor's deceased wife Hope often met him after work. Trevor quickly rushed to grab it, placing his bag beside him to reserve the seat for someone he expected. The park was always better than his apartment, where signs of his wife were everywhere.

Trevor opened the bag, his hand revealing also many scars, and pulled out earphones and a music player. He searched on the player for Pergolesi's "Stabat Mater," a piece he always played when his spirits were low. His eyes closed. A deep breath of the freshly mowed grass entered his nostrils. For a blessed few minutes, the music was a distraction. It blocked the sounds of sirens, gunfire, screaming, crying, people yelling "help, help, please help me," and the image of Hope and him on fire.

Someone approached and bumped into the bench. For a second Trevor believed it was Hope. She would often tease him by creeping up on him and say in a disguised voice, "Is anyone sitting here? Are you waiting for anyone?" He would say, "Yes, I'm sorry, I'm waiting for someone." But now he was indeed waiting. She would never join him.

He would wait forever. The thought made his lips tremble and his eyes redden.

Trevor wiped the tears away with his coat sleeve.

A man was standing at the end of the bench wearing sunglasses and a wide hat that hid a face covered with bruises and cuts, and a swollen lip and eye. Trevor moved his bag to make room for him.

The man sat down without speaking.

"Mohammed," Trevor greeted him.

Mohammed reached out, slowly patted Trevor's shoulders a few times in a gesture of greeting and reassurance, sat down, and took out a brown papered covered book from his backpack. Very quietly he began reading out loud in a chant-like rhythm in Arabic.

Trevor also restarted his music, but the images of the darkly lit floor at the vast cave-like club Locals Only had already gripped his mind and were preventing him from experiencing the music. With couples dancing, different colored lights flashing, a band playing at one end, a bar along one side, people one moment laughing and enjoying themselves, the next moment scrambling to the exits, pushing and stepping on one another, shouting, "Move! Get out of the way!" with no explanation, a row of men in masks appeared holding in their hands guns and equipment of some sort while another group dragged Hope and other women and lined them up against the wall. Trevor could hear himself yelling, "No!" while a flamethrower sprayed the women with a fire while the attackers shouted "whore" and "slut."

Trevor and several men rushed forward to attempt to save their wives, girlfriends, and friends, but it was too late. Once the women were on fire, the attackers shot them all. That's when he saw himself in the mirrors that covered the walls of the club. He was lifting and holding Hope in his arms, Hope and he engulfed in flames, and, at the same time, from the corner of his eye, the police entering the door, and himself collapsing to the floor, Hope falling on him but still in his arms.

Trevor turned up the volume of the "Stabat Mater" to attempt to blare out the images and sounds in his head while looking at Mohammed repeating verses from the Koran.

Mohammed's eyes and face were now wet. Like Trevor with the "Stabat Mater," Mohammed believed the reading of the Koran would help him overcome his loss. The image of his beloved sister Zorah was stamped on his consciousness. Zorah had come with two of her female friends to Locals Only to dance. She had just called her brother to come pick her up when the attackers arrived. That was the last time Mohammed spoke with her. When he arrived at the club, police, fire engines and ambulances had blocked off the area, and the street was filled with covered burnt bodies neatly lying in rows.

A group of grieving men ran over to Mohammed's car.

"This is your doing," one of them blared, pounding the hood of his car. "What's wrong with you people?"

They dragged him from his car and began kicking and hitting him in his head until the police intervened.

Trevor had not witnessed the beating of Mohammed and other Muslim men that night. An ambulance was taking him to the hospital. His first meeting with Mohammed was in the support group of family and friends of those killed at the club. Mohammed sat next to him in a fully bandaged face and a sling around his arm.

Images of his dead sister and the threats to him and his community forced Mohammed to stop reciting. Covering his eyes, he broke down into a muffled cry, trying his best to conceal his emotion. His arm began to shake.

Trevor grabbed Mohammed's arm and held it until the shaking stopped.

A slight breeze appeared. Dogs were barking. Two squirrels were chasing after each other down into the gully. Behind Trevor and

Mohammed, a family was playing a board game. On the baseball field, the crack of the bat hitting the ball and team members shouting out support to each other filtered through the park. Fifty feet away an elderly couple sat on a bench in a similar position facing the gully. They stared forward without words or visible emotion, sharing decades of memories of sitting in their spot. Occasionally Trevor would look over at them in envy.

Trevor and Mohammed spoke very little to each other. It felt good to be out of their homes, in the fresh air, and have someone else beside them who had a similar experience.

They had peace for an hour. No one noticed them until two young men heard Mohammed chanting, rushed at him, grabbed his Koran, threw it into the gully, and pushed Mohammed to the ground.

Trevor stood up when he witnessed this action and quickly removed his hat, coat, and T-shirt to show his badly burned and disfigured body. The sight of the body not only shocked the harassers but revealed the man whose photo was in every newspaper and whom the media had interviewed. In person the physical damage was more horrible than the images they had seen of Trevor on TV, making Trevor appear more like a monster than a human.

"Why are you sitting with him?" they asked. "It's people like him who killed your wife and made you look like this."

Trevor immediately went down the hill to fetch the Koran.

When he returned, after brushing the dirt and debris off the book, he handed the Koran to Mohammed, but said nothing to those harassing Mohammed. Instead Trevor helped Mohammed to his feet and back to the bench, where they continued with their private mourning.

The attackers seemed prepared to continue their harassment when two policemen arrived.

By now people in the park had heard that there was an incident involving a Muslim and the badly burned man from the attack at Locals Only. Very soon afterwards, the elderly couple deserted their favorite bench. The families nearby gathered their belongings and quickly left. Others too had the same idea and were preparing to exit. The baseball game stopped.

The police suggested to Mohammed that he should not risk staying.

Trevor accompanied Mohammed in protest, his shirt and hat still off to bring attention to the situation, hoping the media would broadcast or write about it.

Once they had departed, the people returned and soon were once again enjoying themselves under a bright hot sun and cloudless sky.

THE END

Falcons

The process of adopting Isabel was lengthy and unusual. The birth mother wavered on whether to give the child up and insisted on meeting the parents, William and Donna, a demand that had to be completed secretly because the rules forbid it. After this difficulty was resolved, the birth mother also expected extra monies to release the child.

The adoption was finally approved. On that day the birth mother gave to Isabel two gifts, both symbolic of Isabel's origins. The first was a local exotic plant that was the national plant and filled the garden of Isabel's birth mother. The second was a doll dressed in the folk costume of Isabel's homeland with several different animals on the dress that were indigenous. Isabel loved the doll and daily begged her parents to identify each of the animals by name as a kind of ritual before Isabel went to sleep. The exotic plant was placed prominently on the kitchen table.

*

In only a few years, both Isabel and William died from the same cause, poison.

Isabel died in the hospital with only Donna beside her because William was so distraught by Isabel's sickness that he had to be hospitalized for acute depression and shock.

While sitting at the edge of the bed, Donna heard Isabel say in a voice without a hint of fear,

"Am I really going to die, Mommy?"

Donna could not speak. She could not say the words. She just nodded.

"Isn't there a way for them to save me? They saved Margery."

Isabel pointed to the girl in the bed diagonal across from her.

Donna shook her head.

"I'm so sorry, sweetie."

She leaned over the bed and hugged her.

Isabel had looked at herself in the mirror and did not think she would die. She appeared healthy. But her mother said Isabel would die and her mother would not lie.

"That's OK, Mommy," Isabel said to Donna, again in a calm tone. "Don't worry. You'll be all right."

Donna, who treasured her daughter beyond description, was trying to control her distress, but when her daughter said this last statement, the gulp in her throat, the water behind her eyes, and the pressure in her lungs and stomach, burst. She hurriedly left the room and, unseen by her daughter, let out as much emotion as she could, the tears flowing quickly and heavily. Her body tightened so much she could not breath and her chest was heaving from the sobs.

When Donna returned to the room, her eyes now red and her face flush, she decided to be honest about her feelings with her daughter, even though this idea went against her common sense. She did not want Isabel to die without realizing how much her parents loved her.

"I won't be all right, Isabel. I will never be all right. I would do anything to save you. I love you, my little darling, so much I want to die with you. I do."

Donna repeated the words under her breath. "I want to die with you, I do."

"But we'll see each other in heaven, right?" Isabel said with a smile. "Daddy says he'll talk about the animals on my blouse even in heaven. How soon will I see you and Daddy after I die?"

"You won't even know, it will be so quick," Donna said, with as much encouragement as she could find, her words breaking up, the tears now falling down her cheeks again. "In no time Daddy and I will join you and we'll once again talk about the animals on the blouse. It will seem like a minute."

Isabel laughed and reached out her thin small arms for a hug and Donna grabbed her baby and squeezed her tight.

"I'm so glad you have Daddy," Isabel whispered and assured Donna.

Donna nodded.

The hug and whispers were the last goodbyes in Isabel's brief life. Soon after Isabel's body went limp and stopped moving and breathing.

Donna prized that conversation with her daughter so much that she repeated it numerous times over the years. At least she had the opportunity to talk with Isabel and assure her. At least Isabel had talked with her mother before she passed away. Even in death there can be positives.

There were no positives to the death of her husband William. Two weeks after the death of Isabel, they found his body at work, his head on the desk, and a list she had given him that morning beside his head on which were the words: Bread, Milk, Fruit, Beans, and Coffee, plus two words he had added, See and Falcons. That was it. No prior sicknesses, no months or years of illness, no warning, and no final conversation. Donna buried him within a week.

Isabel and her father died from the poison of the same exotic plant, the plant that the birth mother had given them as a parting gift. How William and Isabel each ingested the poison was a mystery at the time. Evidently, he died shortly after writing "see" and "falcons," since the pen fell on the floor and the last word "falcons" was barely legible when the poison overwhelmed him.

The words baffled Donna. On the day he died, he had been eating lunch at the park. Had he seen falcons at the park? Falcons were common in the park. Why would he make note of it? The police saw nothing of importance in the words and, with no leads, closed both cases. Without more information, they had no lines of investigation. The detective assumed that a poison leaf from the plant had somehow fallen into a liquid both of them were drinking.

*

Donna chose to trudge on with her life and let the razors of heartache and loss cut away at her spirit and turn her into a bitter and angry woman. She finished a college program and found a job. The studies and job were not pleasurable, but they were something to keep her busy. Her parents and friends were pressuring her to meet someone else, start a new life, and put the past behind her, but as the years passed they all relented. She could not end her bond with Isabel and William or forget the connection of the plant and her loved ones, especially because the plant was a gift from the birth mother.

Donna turned on God. Why was she chosen for this suffering? What could she have done that could force, in a skewed universe and an unfeeling God, this retribution? She couldn't believe God would take such revenge on her, but she couldn't find any other reason for this misery. Who else could she blame? There were nights when she searched her past life to find that reason for this punishment, but she discovered nothing. She had been, in her opinion, a good person.

One evening she sat in her living room, repeating what had become the same ritual. Barber's "Adagio for Strings" was playing quietly. The fire was happily and slowly killing the logs. A glass of wine awaited on the table before her. Resting beside her, snuggled up tightly, was Isabel's favorite doll. Only the light of the fire lit the room.

While staring at the fire, she opened a box and removed the precious note. Tears immediately came, she whimpered a little, and then wiped her face. She read it aloud: "Bread, Milk, Fruit, Beans, Coffee, See, Falcons." William knew he was dying and could barely complete the last words.

Donna enjoyed massaging the paper of the note, thinking always how he had held it in his hands and repeating the final words he wrote just after, she assumed, he came from his lunch at the park and had his usual coffee. There was no cup in his office, so the police assumed he left it at the park.

She often imagined his last hours. The park must have been filled with people of different ages, most of them probably joyful. There were young mothers with their babies and children, older and younger single people sitting on benches looking at books or pressed up against each other, people eating at the picnic benches, feeding the birds, smiles, laughter, and some walking, and bicycling. There sitting high in the trees or flying perhaps were a few falcons. The scene must have been inspiring and satisfying. William must have had a sense of contentment, even though he was still in deep grief about Isabel.

Nevertheless, the connection of the words "see" and "falcons" eluded her. She could not understand why he had used that simple phrase or those words. What was he trying to write? Why would he note that he had seen falcons? Why did he feel compelled to write them down when he was dying?

That night, as she finished her ritual and was preparing to go to sleep, she set the doll on Isabel's chair next to the bed and, as always, when she looked at the doll, for a minute focused on its blouse covered by animals. These were the animals that each night Isabel wanted her parents to discuss before she went to sleep. Though there were many types of animals, most of them were falcons.

Donna gasped and started to walk furiously around the room. She had come to a startling conclusion.

*William was trying to send a message. He was trying to tell me
that Isabel's birth mother had killed him and Isabel. Yes, that had
to be it. I knew it! That woman never wanted us to have Isabel.
William and she must have had a conversation at the park. The
birth mother had somehow dipped a leaf from the poisonous plant
into his coffee at the park; he realized he was going to die, and he
wrote hurriedly what would point to his killer, especially something
that he did every night when he put Isabel to sleep; he would talk
about the birds on the blouse. In those few seconds, he wrote the
word "see" and could not add "the birth mother," there were too
many words, he was too weak and dying, but did write "falcons"
because he thought I would recognize the word "falcon." He could
not write "doll" because Isabel had other dolls. He never had the
chance to write more. But he wanted me to look at the blouse with
the falcons, and how they came to have the doll. "See" the one
who gave Isabel the doll with the "falcons" on her blouse and this
meant: see the one who poisoned William and Isabel. It was the
best he could muster and did not have a clear head.*

That series of events became more and more plausible to the
obsessed and grieving mind of Donna, but she knew that the police
would not consider it sufficient proof. Even if they did, they would not
execute her; they would give her a life sentence. That punishment, to
Donna, would not fit the crime.

She decided that this revelation was God at work.

*This was God's work of justice. God had waited until now to
reveal this fact to me after the investigation was over. God did not
want the killer to be caught and remain in a prison cell. God was
asking me to do the work of justice.*

After searching for the birth mother for a year. Donna secretly
broke into her apartment and squeezed a little juice from a leaf into a
quart of milk in the mother's refrigerator. Isabel's birth mother died that

same evening. Authorities would soon link the death to the deaths of William and Isabel because the plant was so rare in Donna's country. But no evidence linked Donna with the murder.

After killing the birth mother, Donna herself was ready to die. She wanted God to strike her with lightning, stop her grieving heart, plan an accident, or give her cancer. Anything! It was up to God, but Donna believed she deserved to die. She wanted to join her husband and daughter. There was no reason to live. When she looked at the note and the doll and thought how the Isabel's birth mother had schemed to ruin her life by giving that plant, how she poisoned William at the park while he innocently had his lunch break, and how that woman killed her own child rather than let Isabel grow up and have her own life, a woman who would kill to stop another's happiness, Donna would scream out in anger at the world and the great injustice for which there was no recompense, even after brutal years of pain.

Yet Donna lived on into her nineties.

God had swooped down and taken the joy from my life. God will give me no relief. He wants me to relive every day the pains of my loss.

*

When Donna finally passed away, the police received a note in which she confessed that she had killed the birth mother and the reason she had killed her. They also found the box Donna opened each night. Inside were now not one but two notes. The first note was the one found on William's desk at work that listed the words, Bread, Milk, Fruit, Beans, Coffee, See, and Falcons. The second note Donna had discovered days before her own death. It was a note that had fallen into a crevice in the back of the dresser and had remained there for all the years of Donna's bitter suffering. William had written it before he had gone to work on the day he died. It said:

"Please forgive me, my love, but Isabel died because of me. While I was reading the newspaper, a tiny leaf fell into her juice and I found it later at the bottom of her glass. I would have seen it fall if I had been paying attention. I immediately removed it and flushed it down the toilet. I am so distraught. I can't live thinking my negligence killed our precious darling. Nor did I have the courage to confess to you. So I have dipped a leaf into my own juice. I will die from the same poison that killed our beautiful little girl. Please place in my casket the doll with the falcons on the dress. I want to see those falcons when I awake in heaven with our little girl. Goodbye, my love. For my sake, please don't let my mistake keep you from your deserved happiness."

THE END

When You Shoot an Arrow

"When you shoot an arrow, it will go where you shoot it. You control the arrow because you control the bow. Don't place guilt on the arrow or the bow if you can't see the target. You aim the arrow, not some ghost. Otherwise, don't pick up the bow. Wait for the archer."

That's what my father told me when I was twelve years old. I had no idea what he meant because I never talked about archery, never shot an arrow; and, as far as I knew, he had never owned a bow or shot an arrow. And what did he mean by a ghost? What ghost?

I recall those sentences because my father disappeared a week later. The police tried to find him or his body, but they closed the case after a couple of years. They believed that he was either killed or abducted because there was no indication he wanted to leave his family: he had a good job as a mechanic, had a circle of friends, showed no signs of depression, and had a good marriage. I refuse to think he would plan to desert us, and if he did, he would not leave us with no financial resources. My Mom was working at the time in a beauty salon, but her wages were too low. A few days after my Dad disappeared someone out of the blue offered her an excellent job as a waitress at a high-volume restaurant and bar. We were much more secure after that.

I have only good memories about my father, but I thought mostly about why he left. Only two facts about his disappearance I recall from that time. The first were the words I have mentioned about the bow and arrow. The second was a piece of information my mother gave to the police. My father told my mother about a group called the Whisper People. There was no information about the Whisper People on the Internet. According to my mother, he claimed he met them in the parking garage under the City Hall. I expected him to say he met them in the canyons or the mountains or the unexplored forests or jungles or in a temple, or somewhere mystical or mysterious. In any case, he gave no sign that they were coercing him in any way. They wanted him to "discover his emptiness, silence, and inaction," concepts that were an enigma to me.

The police said, in one of many possibilities, that the so-called Whisper People threatened to hurt my mother and me if he did not join them. Paradoxically I hoped that was the case because, regardless what happened, I did not want to learn that my father was dead. I hoped that somehow, some day, he would return or I or someone else would find him.

My mother waited ten years for him to walk in the door before she married another. I was twenty-two years old when she met someone. I'm not sure she was in love, but she had to go on with her own life now that her son had grown up. Everyone said to my Mom and me to close the book that concerned my father. Good memories of him would always remain. Love from that time would stay in our hearts. Time to start a new book.

Anyone who has had this experience will know that no book of life is closed, however much you want to close it, especially when it was such a heart-warming book. The truth of why he left and other unanswered questions plague you. If he was abducted, where is he now? Where does he live? What does he do to survive? Assuming the Whisper People did coerce him, what do the Whisper People do and what do they think? Why would the Whisper People want my father?

To this last question my mother had a partial answer. He was, she told me, a tireless seeker into the ineffable, and that was one of the reasons she loved him. He claimed to have had many strange, spiritual experiences that scared her but comforted him. When he read, he read about religion, mysticism and spirituality. Representatives of many groups visited him. Though his job was a car mechanic, his life was about the mysteries. In this light, she was not surprised that one group of the many he knew would gravitate to him or that he would want to join them. The difference was that she never met or learned anything about the Whisper People.

The image of my father soon transformed from a normal Dad to a legend and myth. Those words about the bow and the Whisper People had become a bothersome puzzle. I tried every crazy idea to determine what happened, even spending hours hanging out at the parking garage under the City Hall, hoping someone from the Whisper People would contact me. The police had tried this idea after the abduction, but I assumed that the Whisper People would stay away from them. Perhaps now they would return.

They did not.

After no success, I became discouraged and depressed. My hope had faded away. I had been shooting plenty of arrows, but not hitting any targets. My mother herself said that I should move on and not worry about what had happened to him.

*

I had managed to lessen my obsession for a while when a well-dressed woman with two powerfully built men on each side of her approached me at the community center, where I was playing table tennis.

She said in a commanding voice, as if I was trying to obstruct or hide something from her,

"Where's your father?"

Naturally I stopped playing and stared at this person I had never met.

"I'm sorry," I said, in a cold tone. "Who are you?"

Her question I had been asked many times since I was twelve years old. It only reminded me of that hole in my life.

"That doesn't matter. Where's your father?"

"I don't know," I curtly replied and returned to playing. "I haven't seen him since I was twelve."

"Stop this nonsense!" she said and grabbed my paddle. "I've been searching for two years. I know you're his son. He must communicate with you."

I stopped playing and asked if she would join me at a table in the corner.

Her name, I learned, was Emilia von Gorsdale. The Gorsdales— the "von" part the family bought—were one of the richest families in the world and had been wealthy for many generations. With such resources, I later realized, it was no surprise she was able to find me.

"You knew my father?" I asked. "You knew my father two years ago?"

"Yes."

"You had conversations with him?" I asked, becoming very excited.

"I had a lot of conversations with him."

"I'm sorry," I told her, "but I have no idea where he is. We think he may have been taken by or joined the Whisper People."

"Ah, the Whisper People. I remember him mentioning them."

"Where did you first meet him?" I asked.

"In Venice. At a Vivaldi festival. He asked me if he could sit in the front row, even though I had bought out the whole row for privacy. I agreed, but I did not expect that he would sit down next to me. He never said a word during the concert, but at the end thanked me and said I had two different ears, one attached, one unattached.

"'It's a genetic feature of my family,' I told him.

"Then he showed me his ears. He too had the same kind of ears.

"We both laughed.

"'Nonetheless, madam,' he said, 'that's peculiar. What else is peculiar about you?'

"'Oh, a great deal,' I said.

"And we laughed again.

"'You're an interesting person,' he said. 'I'd like to know why. Can I meet you at the Monteverdi opera next week?'

"And he left before I could give him an answer.

"He did go to the opera as he said. I didn't go but I sent one of my friends. Your father sat motionless through the concert, apparently transfixed by the music and story.

"At the end, my friend handed him my card with the address of a small café hidden in one of the many alleys of Venice, a café that I had reserved for the night, not for meeting him, but so that I could have privacy with my friends and family.

"Your father came to the café and sat down.

"Now, let me say this before I tell you anything more. Prior to meeting your father, my life had for several years been a series of escapes from or avoidance of annoying people. No one wanted to know me, they wanted my money or connections, to rob me, in a nice way. So when I heard that this man wanted to know me, just me, I admit I was strangely intrigued.

"'I won't tell you a thing about myself, sir,' I said initially, 'unless you tell me about you. As you can see, I have guards at the door and won't hesitate to call them if there is any impropriety. Who are you?'

"Your father focused on me and said, 'I'm one of the Whisper People.'

"'That tells me nothing,' I said, 'because I know nothing about them. Who are you?'

"'I'm here to find out about you.' he said.

"'Where do you come from?' I asked.

"'I was married and had a child,' he replied. 'I became one of the Whisper People. There's nothing more to know about me.'

"'What are your hobbies? You clearly like music. Do you like any sports? What books do you read? Do you travel? What jobs have you had? Things like that. Tell me, so I can know you better.'

"Your father stood up and with a much firmer tone said: 'I'm unimportant. There's nothing to be gained by knowing about my past. Let me understand you, please. If this is unacceptable, I will leave.'

"Again I was lured by his curiosity about me and decided to meet with him.

"We met in the café for many weeks, talking, my guards always nearby, and I let him ask me an endless series of questions about how I came to be who I was, why I did what I did, what my life meant, and why I thought this way or that about a hundred different things. Never had anyone had such a fascination with me without an ulterior motive, and, to be honest, after spending so many hours with him in the café, I truly felt I was in fact interesting but also empty, knowledgeable but mostly ignorant, and, most important, I couldn't support very well anything I did, believed, thought, or was. All of my assumptions were refutable.

"Then one day he never showed at a meeting and I couldn't find him."

"What did you do?" I asked. "And why did he leave?"

"I never learned why he vanished. But what did I do? Frankly I did nothing. I was lost. So many questions remained unanswered. I guess I thought he would always be there. Eventually I realized that I had to rebuild my entire being from the ground up. Believe me, it's challenging work, and I needed his help. I remember his last question: How is the best way to remain silent and not move?"

She stopped to grab a tissue from her purse and pat her eyes, which were tearing up.

"Did you learn anything about the Whisper People?" I asked.

She shook her head.

"He only mentioned them once, at the beginning. I asked about them, but he always had the same answer: 'Our focus is on you, not on me or them.'

"How did he earn a living?" I asked.

"I don't know. He never asked for money. He never asked for anything. From what I could gather, this was his work. I do know how he found out about me. He had heard about me from Bart Fellows, who also, he said, has ears like mine. I immediately called Bart, but he only told me what I already knew."

As I looked at her now red eyes, I not only sympathized with her, but all my own regret and frustrations welled up again.

"I have searched every transit system in every nation," she said in a tired, agonizing tone, "every footpath, every airline, every road that leaves Venice and Italy, but with no results. I hired an entire detective agency to find him, using his DNA, but so far only you have turned up. I wonder now if he ever existed at all. I mean, who goes around questioning people like that? You're my last hope. I'm praying that one of these days he'll contact you. If he does, here's my card."

I took the card and strangely felt happy on some level. For twelve years I had searched without success. But now I discovered that my father had been alive two years ago!

I immediately told my mother and informed the police. They re-opened the case and contacted the Italian authorities.

*

My own search began again. I first went to see Bart Fellows, a lawyer who quit the law and now ran a refuge for abused, disabled, or unwanted animals in upstate New York, in the United States.

His report was similar to Emilia's story. My Dad would spend the entire time asking him questions, such as "Why do you do this, Bart? What's driving you? Tell me about the emotions you feel when you help one of these little creatures? How did you get like this, with so much empathy?" With question after question he would try to draw from Bart the feelings and passions behind Bart's work and why he thought the way he did. Bart told me it was enlightening, but also tiresome and frustrating. Yet because of my Dad's sincerity, he could never refuse. It seemed to Bart as if he was desperate to understand why Bart existed, as if he must know or there would be consequences for my father.

Somewhere in their conversation—Bart could not remember where—Bart had mentioned Emilia, never thinking he would pursue her. But after visiting him perhaps a dozen times, without mentioning the Whisper People, my father again vanished and never returned.

Bart believed that my father heard about Bart through his fiancé, Sophia Wicksome, a professional ballet dancer who ended the engagement after Bart's decision to move to a rural location and quit his profession as a lawyer. Sophia also had attached and unattached earlobes.

I tracked Sophia Wicksome to New Delhi, where she was an instructor with the National Ballet Academy, teaching Western ballet to the young people of India. My father spent much more time with her than with Bart, but there was little difference in his method. He wanted to know what compelled her to dance, what she felt about the dance, and what she had sacrificed to become a dancer. Then he asked her to break down, step by step, how she would feel emotionally when she dance a dance, for example, in "Swan Lake" or one of Balanchine's ballets.

I met Sophia at a café near the ballet academy. At first she was nervous and said she would rather not open that period of her life.

"Did he hurt you?" I asked.

"Hurt me? Well yes, I suppose he did, but I suppose I needed the hurt."

Sophia said his probing questions about why she was a dancer, what she thought about dancing, and what dance was, created over time an eerie state of mind in her, as if on each visit she was leaving her body and looking at herself being grilled. His focus on her choices and her inner needs seemed almost maniacal. Some nights she had nightmares after visiting with him. She could never quench his curiosity, as if some inner demon fed on her answers.

Once he exhausted dance, he then began asking the same questions he asked Emilia and Bart, questions about what she assumed about life and herself. These too became so traumatic that finally she could not bear to see him.

"Why didn't you refuse to answer, why not send him away?" I asked.

She smiled.

"That tactic may work when you're young and have never lived. But when revelations begin to pore out of you, struggles you've been dealing with since your youth, the questions become a kind of drug that you need. I couldn't stop. I wanted to know more and more about me. I wanted to find the answers as much as he did."

"What did you do? How did you break free?"

"Well, I confess—because what I did wasn't kind—I turned him on Bart, that Bart needed him more. I'm sorry I had to do it. I swear, I was going to have a nervous breakdown. Please. I'd rather not talk about it anymore."

I apologized for upsetting her. We talked no more about her conversations, but Sophia did give me a link to other people my father knew in India, one of whom was William Kelley, an honorary member of the ballet's board of directors. My father met him at one of the meetings at which Sophia was giving a presentation. Kelly was a member of parliament who was working with the Indian government at the time. My father followed William back to England before he went on to Bart. Kelley also had similar ears as Sophia, Bart, and Emilia.

I sat down on the couch in Kelley's living room. At first his wife seemed suspicious of me, as if I was a kind of advance scout for my father. I assured I wasn't associated with my father and hadn't seen him in many years. On the contrary, I was trying to find him.

"Oh you don't want to find him!" his wife exclaimed. "No, no. You want to stay away from him. That man is a…a…a sorcerer."

"Well, not exactly," Kelly said, smiling. "Look, in those days I was accustomed to some pretty odd characters in my constituency and was obliged to tolerate them all, but your father? Honestly I never met anyone like that fellow. At first I found his probing questions interesting and engaging. He and I analyzed matters about my life I had taken for granted, including reasons for why I decided to be in government. But as the weeks went on, I found this incessant baring of my soul far too complicated and depressing if I was to continue in my present work. You see, he had a way of exposing the falsity of one's motives and the true reasons why you made certain choices. It was not comfortable, I can tell you. Yet it was addictive, as if you were coming to know yourself. But my wife told me it was too late for self-examination, that he created a battle zone in which I had not enough weapons to survive. Your father made me doubt the purity of my motivations and he did it with such gentleness and kindness, as if it was OK to throw your life away. Why did I choose government as a career? How would I decide to support a particular policy, party, position, individual, organization, potential law, budget item, and so on? What did I think about government as a system? Oh, I don't know. There were so many. None of these conversations touched on any confidential matter. The inner forces of choice were his focus, centered around how I became the man I was."

"No one should know himself that well!" Kelley's wife proclaimed. "You do what you do."

But, nonetheless, like Sophia, the interrogation about how he became an M.P. or how he came to his assumptions began to destabilize his attitudes toward himself and his work. His wife told William to break off the conversations, but, like others, William was losing his will. He could not resist. The probing and questioning began to change him and the fog in which he had once lived floated away, leaving a clarity that was almost horrifying.

"Get to the point, Will," his wife said. "As a result of that man, Will resigned. Resigned! He resigned from his position. He quit! But did that stop your father?"

"He wanted to know the answer to the key question:" Will said. "What was the meaning of my existence? It may seem like not an earth-shaking question, but after the weeks of probing, I literally could not move. I was…paralyzed. I could not function."

William let him in the house one day but could not stay near him. William rushed out of the room, while his wife firmly told my father she never wanted to see his face again.

They were glad to see me go also.

Unfortunately, none of these people knew anything about the Whisper People or personal details about my father beyond his technique of incessant questioning. Did the Whisper People actually exist? Once again, I was at an impasse. I was no closer to finding my father. I needed to determine what person he now was pursuing.

I called Emilia. Only two people still alive had come up in her conversations with my father. Both she had contacted and had placed under surveillance. One had refused to see him, and other was her brother, Professor Andre von Gorsdale at the University of Paris, a specialist in Leibniz.

I thanked her and decided to go to Paris and monitor the professor's residence and office myself. It is possible, I said, that he had noted the detectives and stayed away. Perhaps he will feel differently about his son.

On one evening I was watching Emile's office, sitting on a bench in a small courtyard eating a croissant and drinking coffee. The courtyard had a tiny garden and in the center was a statue of Minerva, goddess of education. There was a single light over the courtyard, but it hardly lit the area in this night because clouds covered the moon. Yet the bench gave me a good sightline to see who came to the professor's office.

A figure in a long gold robe sat down next to me with a face concealed behind a hood. The figure startled me. I instinctively rose to leave.

"Why are you here?" he asked as I rose.

"Pardon me," I replied, turning back to face him.

"I've seen you out here for a long time," he said. "You come, you sit, you seem to wait, and then you leave."

I was unsure what to say.

"Are you Professor von Gorsdale?" I asked.

"No, I'm not."

"I wanted to meet him," I explained.

"What do you do?" he asked.

The question irritated me, I don't know why. It seemed so unusual for a conversation between two strangers.

I began to walk away, not answering his question.

"Are you afraid to tell me what you do?"

I stopped and turned around, facing him again.

"I'm a poet," I said. "What do you do?"

"I'm an archer," he said.

The implication of that answer was too obvious for me to miss.

"I shoot arrows," he added. "But enough about me. Please come, sit, and talk to me about you. You seem like an interesting fellow, wanting to talk to a professor who's a specialist in Leibniz. Do you also study Leibniz?"

I knew his routine of interrogation and wasn't going to be roped in by it.

"Could I first ask some questions about you?" I asked.

"Oh, my life is quite boring," he responded. "I was once married, had a son. I'm one of the Whisper People."

"The Whisper People?" I said quizzically. "Never heard of them."

"There are very few of us, only around three hundred in the whole world. We're aliens."

I froze. I thought: What? Aliens? Aliens? This man, my father, is mentally ill. He thinks he's an alien?

"I'm sure you're surprised to hear that," he added. "Perhaps you don't believe it. That's fine."

"What do you do?" I asked hesitantly, not sure I wanted to be talking on a dark evening with a person in a golden hood and robe who seemed like a character from another time and who claimed to be an alien.

"We create webs of self-truth, we're archers who help others aim for and reach targets. It's an art. It's our way to survive."

Already he told me more than he had told any of the others. Who else knew he was an archer or an alien? Did he suspect I was his son?

He smiled.

"But you are not part of my web," he said, laughing. "Professor von Gorsdale is."

"Why not me?"

"There are a couple of reasons, but they are unimportant. You have no connection to the strands of my web. I work only with those in my web. We must remain in our webs and create strong strands by intensive interrogation. Self-examination strengthens our webs."

I laughed even harder than he.

"I have a greater connection than any of them!" I proudly informed him. "Don't you know I'm your son?"

Surprisingly he did not react as if he was pleased or not.

After a pause, he said: "you're not part of my web."

His lack of response in acknowledging I was his son appalled me. Partly in anger and partly because of disappointment, I quickly rose and walked away, without looking back.

After I had walked for a few minutes, I calmed myself and realized I needed to ask more questions of him.

I went back to the bench.

He was gone.

On the bench was an arrow with a note wrapped around it. The note said:

Prepare yourself. Become the archer. Remember: When you shoot an arrow, do not pick the easy target. Do not seek the parent. Do not aim at ghosts. Place your target as far as possible in the distance and practice carefully, as often as possible, aiming and shooting. Look for what is difficult and strange, as if you were shooting through the woods in the dark. Know the arrow and become the target.

THE END

Freckled Woman

On a hot summer day, the Salinas Gallery was showing John Andrea's super-realistic sculpture, "Freckled Woman," a full-size nude sculpture of a young woman. Numerous people, glad to be in an air-conditioned building, wearing as few clothes as appropriate, were walking around it, observing it from every angle, awestruck at the incredible ability of the artist to reproduce the skin and anatomy of a human body, with every curve, bump, mole, wrinkle, and, in this case, freckles. Observers expected at any moment for the sculpture to stop its frozen pose and walk away, as if it was a mime. Though a sign asked viewers not to touch the sculpture, several could not resist; they needed to prove to themselves that her "flesh" had no warmth. Many looked away when their eyes met the sculpture's eyes, wondering if a real being was entombed underneath the manufactured skin.

"My god, you're right, it looks just like you!" Becca said to her friend Victoria, both dressed in shorts and halter tops but still not yet cooled off from the blistering heat outside. "That's your face, your dimple, your triple earrings in the left ear."

"Now do you believe me?!" Victoria said, her face intentionally veiled by large sunglasses. "Now was the trip worth it? I told you. Even my weird little toe on my right foot."

"Oh my god, look!" Becca added, pointing. "The mole."

"Fine, yes. The mole on my back."

"OK, he had to be at the life class," Becca said, throwing up her arms, "how else could this be? He was there and saw you nude. There's no other explanation, Vicky. Too much detail. After all, he lives in the same city as you."

"No, I checked, twice," Victoria said. "Everyone in there was a painter."

At first the class seemed a possibility. After all, Victoria thought, only in the life class was she nude before strangers, and only the front of her body was seen by the group. How could someone have captured so much detail of the rest of her?

"Someone somehow photographed or videoed you," Becca said, "and sent it to him."

Eventually, the answer lit up Victoria's mind. When she was in university and needed money, a photographer had paid her for several nude shots and she had signed a form that allowed him to sell them. Perhaps he had also made a video without her knowledge. This sculptor had clearly bought these photos or seen a video.

Regardless how it happened, Victoria could not believe the likeness. To see her face and form in sculpture was strange enough. But even more remarkable to Victoria was to look at how the artist had perfectly copied her feet, her neck, her hips, her breasts, her pubic area, her whole figure. It even seemed like her skin. The artist had captured her physical being.

"Unbelievable!" Becca spoke loudly in astonishment. "I mean, I feel like going up and talking to it and saying, 'What's up, Vicky.'"

"Shhh!" Victoria whispered. "Yes, it's me. Except for one big difference."

The "Freckled Woman" had freckles all over her body.

After taking the tour around the sculpture, they found a bench up against the far wall, at the other end from the sculpture.

"What should you do?" Becca asked quietly. "Sue him? He's exposing you. To everyone! Thank god this show is a thousand miles away. If this was shown at home in a local gallery or museum, everyone would know it was you. Think what your parents would say."

Victoria smiled.

"I'm jealous of the attention the sculpture gets from that guy."

"Who?" Becca asked. "

"That guy sitting right in front of the sculpture!"

"That cute guy with black hair?"

"Uh-huh."

Victoria was staring at the tall and lanky Andrew, who saw the photo of the sculpture in the newspaper a month before the exhibition came to town and nervously waited each day for the show to open. When it finally arrived, he lingered at the gallery during its open hours and pined for the sculpture in the night when it was closed.

The "Freckled Woman" fascinated him. To Andrew this was not a sculpture. He called it "she" and "her." He imagined her during every waking hour and dreamed of her in his sleep. His girlfriend tired of hearing about the show and broke up with him.

"It's a sculpture, for god's sake," his father said. "Get over it."

"No," Andrew disagreed, "she's more than that. She's a prophetess, a beautiful warning, encased by our inane world. She screams out: Beware the emptiness."

"What's wrong with you?" his father continued. "I told your mother over and over. Too many books, culture, and reflection. You live in your mind."

Victoria stood up from the bench.

"C'mon. Let's go. I've had enough. I'll return this evening."

"What about the guy?" Becca asked.

"He never takes his eyes off the sculpture."

They left the gallery and went out for dinner.

*

It was a half-hour from closing when Victoria returned by herself, not only to stare again at her sculptural self, but also to look at Andrew, with whom she wanted to find some way of starting a conversation, perhaps go for a coffee, or at least get him to look at her.

At this late hour, only Victoria, the guard, and Andrew were in the room with the sculpture. Most of the lights were off except for one that focused on the "Freckled Woman." The lack of light and people, the eerie silence, made the presence of the sculpture more startling. Victoria almost felt embarrassed for it, and vicariously saw herself standing nude in front of people all day, hoping now that someone might throw a drape over herself.

Victoria chose a long bench that faced the sculpture from the side— the side that showed the mole on her back—and pretended to read about the sculpture in the program. She hung her head low and placed ear phones in her ears without listening to any music. Her focus was on Andrew, to see if he ever looked in her direction.

Andrew never glanced at Victoria. His gaze was fully on the "Freckled Woman."

What was he seeing? she thought. What was he thinking when he ogles my face and body?

Victoria walked behind the sculpture so that he could more easily see her.

Andrew did not change his focus, as if Victoria was invisible.

Victoria intentionally fell to the ground and gave a sound as if she hurt herself.

This fake fall brought both the guard and Andrew to her aid.

"Are you OK?" Andrew said

"What happened?" the guard asked.

"I'm fine," Victoria said. "Nothing. Just clumsy."

Victoria stood up and brushed off the floor dust.

The guard jumped back.

"What? It's incredible," the guard said. He motioned to Andrew. "Look. Look at her. She's...She looks exactly like the sculpture."

Andrew stared for a minute at Victoria, squinted his eyes, and ran over to the sculpture, then back to Victoria.

"Are you aware?" the guard asked Victoria.

She nodded.

"I don't think so," Andrew said. "There's a similarity, but the sculpture is different."

The guard asked her to step inside the ropes and stand next to the sculpture in the same pose. Victoria obliged and posed in the same pose as the sculpture. Victoria was not nude, but her skimpy summer clothes clearly displayed the similarity. The guard took a photo with his cell phone.

"What's your name? I'm going to tell the curator and the critic about you."

Victoria gave her name.

"You're identical!" the guard said.

"The face," Andrew objected, "I agree, has some common features, but I'm not so sure about the body. I mean, the sculpture has freckles and a perfect body."

"Well, I have to close, but this is amazing," the guard said to Victoria. "Please come back tomorrow when the critic is here. He'll be blown away. I mean, the newspapers should hear about this."

After they left the gallery, Victoria said to Andrew:

"I'm Victoria," and reached out her hand.

"Andrew," he replied and shook her hand.

"You come here often?" Victoria asked.

"All day, every day," Andrew said. "I've been waiting for this show for a long time. "I'm...well...I find 'The Freckled Woman' extraordinary."

"The work is extraordinary. And I think you're right, by the way. We are different. I mean, the sculpture and me. "The Freckled Woman," after all, is a sculpture. I'm living."

"She's more than that," Andrew said. "She represents everything."

Victoria nodded.

"Anyway, I gotta go," Andrew said. "Nice to meet you. Goodnight, Victoria."

"Goodnight," Victoria said, as she watched him walked down the street and into the darkness.

*

Victoria told Becca what had happened in a late-night drink at a bar.

"He actually said that?" Becca asked.

"He's obsessed with her," Victoria said.

"'She represents everything,'" Victoria added, trying to duplicate the way he said the words. "I, however, lack the freckles and the perfect body."

"Hey, I've kissed posters on my wall," Becca said.

"How old were you?"

"Good point."

They ordered some guacamole and chips and changed the subject to Becca's decision to get a tattoo. After a half-hour of Victoria assuring Becca she would survive the needles, the conversation returned to the gallery.

"You going back?" Becca asked.

Victoria nodded.

"I can't help myself, I want to look at myself, and I want to see what people say about the sculpture, well, about me. And the sculpture itself has a hold on me. Every comment in some sense is about my face and my body. I heard one woman say that I had the perfect body. Andrew said it too."

"I heard that in high school about you," Becca said.

"Who? You never told me that."

"Making you feel good about your body wasn't on my list in high school. I had my own hang-ups. Anyway, the guys gave you enough compliments."

"Maybe back then. But just so you know, I was never invited back to the figure drawing class. He found someone better. I was too thin, the coordinator said."

"Your breasts could be bigger, I guess," Becca teased. "And then there's the mole. And the weird toe. And let's not forget: the lack of freckles."

"Stop it!"

*

The next day at the Gallery, a prominent art critic was giving his interpretation of the work. The critic, the guard said to Victoria, was made aware of her.

The critic roamed about the sculpture as he spoke, pointing out its features.

"What do we have here? Look at her face. A bored, perhaps even drugged, expression of a young female who has removed her clothes in front of us with no modesty or care for either her body or her self. Notice she has a Brazilian, to erase any sign of maturity. Otherwise, an ordinary young woman—a woman any of us may have seen in our lives—with a form and face that isn't ugly, but lifeless, where the beauty and the positive charge of exuberant life are sucked away. The extreme personification of the sculpture, its actuality, as well as her pose, projects an indolent, empty, and shallow existence, without motion or rhythm, so full of self and indulgence that she can represent only the bareness of her self, only what she superficially is, namely, freckles. At any moment we expect her to take a selfie and put it on the Internet. And what she is, is shown by her lack of any depth outside the surface. She possesses everything but is nothing. Does this sculpture irritate you? It irritates me. I mean, couldn't this be one of our daughters? The message of 'Freckled Woman' is direct: The magic and transcendence in life is gone. Gone! Only desire and pleasure exist, yet even these are fleeting. Her arms hang without significance. The position of her hips is awkward, suggesting again a neutral, dull, and bored sexuality. Innocence has long passed. The materials themselves—polyester resin and fiberglass— indicate a creature who wants to remake nature and life and reality on her own terms."

The critic then stopped and looked out into the audience.

"Is there a woman named Victoria here?" the critic asked. "Could she please come forward?"

Victoria joined him at the front beside the sculpture and removed her sunglasses.

Many members of the audience gasped.

"Hi, Victoria," the critic said. "It's remarkable, looking at you and then at the sculpture. You're identical, and yet you're so different." He asked the audience: "Isn't she?"

The audience indicated that they agreed.

"What do you do, Victoria?"

"I work part-time for Amnesty International and am trying to put myself through law school."

"What do you think of this sculpture? Does it irritate you, on some level?"

"Yes on some level, because it's in my image and that's not how I want to be seen. The artist has taken my persona, manipulated it, and made his own statement."

"Did you pose for the sculptor?" the critic asked.

"Not directly, but yes, I suppose I did," Victoria confessed.

As she was talking, Victoria was looking for Andrew in the audience but could not find him.

*

Later that evening, not too long before the gallery closed, Andrew stood again directly in front of the sculpture.

"You didn't come to the discussion," Victoria said, walking up to him.

"I don't care what he says," Andrew replied. "I have established my own...connection with the 'Freckled Woman.' None of his words could make a difference, one way or the other. I trust my own feelings."

"What do you feel?" Victoria asked.

"That she's entombed in there, chained, and we see the effects of that imprisonment in the way her body poses and her general demeanor. That poor creature is screaming out at us: Don't let them take me! Let me speak! Free me from this empty shell."

For a few moments, they both stared at the sculpture, and Victoria reflected on what he said. His view did not seem that different from what the critic had said.

"What do you think?" Andrew asked.

Victoria had difficulty separating the sculpture from herself. The words of both the critic and Andrew were nudging her away from that identification, but the nakedness of her being was very strong.

"The more I see her," Victoria continued, "the more I see myself, or at least what I think I was. I hope she won't be my future and what I hope to do in my future."

Victoria began to walk away, thinking that Andrew was a lost cause. She could not compete with the sculpture or with how he felt about it. But then an idea occurred to her.

"Look at this," she said, showing her back, which showed the exact mole in the same location as the "Freckled Woman." She also pointed out how her small toe on the right foot curled.

Andrew fell back upon the bench that faced the sculpture.

"You are...you were?"

"Well, no, she's a work of art."

He could not respond.

Victoria gently placed her hand on his bare arm, said good-bye, and walked away.

*

As they were preparing the "Freckled Woman" for shipment, Andrew was there for a final glimpse. The workmen left the sculpture on its back while they went to load other parts of the exhibit on to the truck. Though many times Andrew had wanted to touch the sculpture, he had always controlled himself. Now, believing it would be gone forever, he reached over and touched the sculpture's arm. It was hard and cold. As he did, he recalled how Victoria warm hand had felt on his arm. An odd change in him happened. Now when he looked at the Freckled Woman, he saw Victoria. His vision from the sculpture had vanished.

THE END

The Porch

Werner and Sophia lived in the same rooming house on Charlotte Street for twenty years. Both had never married and both had the same job since they graduated high school. Werner repaired and restored musical instruments and Sophia was a midwife. Over the years they had met this or that potential partner for coffee, rarely for dinner, but neither ever brought someone home to the porch, as the residents called it, the place where you could snuggle and kiss and no one could disturb you. Of course, if no one was romantically using the porch, any of the fifteen residents were welcome to use it. It was far enough from the street so no one could see or hear you, and, in the winter, it could be closed up, heated, and serve also as an excellent place for reading and conversation. The owner of the boarding house, Maria, decorated it with flowers, and placed candles here and there. Even though they might move out as a result, Maria encouraged her residents to seek partners and end their single lives. She even arranged dates for some of them. The porch was part of her strategy, not only for them but for herself.

Werner and Sophia were often on the porch, reading the paper and talking about the news. In fact, they were there together more than any of the other residents. That was not accidental. Werner would secretly wait for Sophia in a corner of the living room and then, as she went toward the porch, he would follow and join her.

"Who you voting for, Sophia?" Werner asked. Werner knew the answer, but it would start a conversation.

"None of your business," Sophia replied.

"It's my business because we're all going to be affected if you vote for Driter. He'll ruin us."

"Oh my Lord, there you go again. Driter is for women and the poor, Werner, and those who need help. That's good enough for me."

"But he's also for big government, spending and waste."

"What are two squabbling about again?" Maria said entering from the house.

"Werner thinks he knows it all," Sophia said. "He's got it all figured out."

"I do not," Werner quickly replied. "I'm going by the liberal's track record. Who you voting for, Maria?"

Maria placed her hands on our apron, pondered the idea a bit, and sat on the steps.

"Not much of a choice, that's all I have to say," Maria finally said. "I'd like to see some controversy, a rabble rouser, someone with some new ideas. After so many years, it's all the same, so boring."

"Well, you have to vote," Sophia said, "like Bishop Tutu said, if you don't vote, oppression wins."

"We don't live under oppression," Werner said.

"Ah, that's your problem," Sophia disagreed. "You don't see it. It sneaks up on ya."

"You two!" Maria said. "Always arguing. Like an old married couple."

"Ha!" Werner said, and laughed. "I wouldn't know, but I sure like arguing with Sophia."

Sophia's phone rang.

"I gotta go," Sophia said.

"Now what?" Maria asked.

"Helena."

"The vomiter?" Maria asked.

"Yep. You know, I love the girl, but I swear she's going to throw up the baby. Her husband's out of town and she thinks she's going to die."

It started to pour.

"Oh boy, now it rains," Sophia realized. "I hate driving in the rain. Why does it always have to rain?"

"I'll drive you," Werner said. "I'm done for the day."

There was a long spell of silence where only the birds hiding in the trees could be heard.

"What do you think, Maria?" Sophia asked. "Shall I give him another chance?"

"What happened anyway?" Maria asked. "I've never heard the whole story."

"Remember Ellen? In the country? Well, my car died, so Mr. Conservative here said he'd drive me. Well, we get there, and it's snowing hard, slippery, and freezing. She's not there. No one's at the farm. No one. I call her and she's at her sister's. I don't recall why. So he takes me to her sister, who's like ten years older than her. And Werner here starts flirting…"

"I was not…" Werner objected.

"Oh yes you were, and she was flirting back, by the way…"

"I was not flirting. We were kidding around."

"So, on the way back I tell him not to behave that way or he'll stay in the car, which normally he does, but it was winter and cold and I felt sorry for him. Well, the flirting bothered my client. I let the rooster in and…"

"Trust me, Maria," Werner said, putting on his coat, "I did no more with her than I do with you.'"

"I beg your pardon," Maria stood up from the step.

"I mean," Werner continued, "I just tease. I had no interest in that woman. C'mon, I tease everybody."

"So a couple of weeks after that," Sophia went on, "I have the same problem with the same dumb car. So Werner drives again. Again it's a storm, same thing all over, and I feel sorry for the guy, so I invite him in again, and again, same story, my client is the wife of a soldier who's overseas, she's staying with her mother, and he chats up the mother…"

"Look, if I liked these women, why didn't I ask them out? I was just being friendly."

"I made a mental note: 'Don't bring Werner along again! Ask Maria to use her car.'"

"OK, I get it," Werner said in an apologetic tone. "I'll stop, I'm really sorry. I'll keep my mouth shut."

Another silence deadened the porch.

"All right, let's go," Sophia said, "you'll get another chance. I'm generous today. You'll stay in the car this time anyway. On our way, Don Juan."

Werner threw up his hands, shook his head, and made a gesture to Maria that Sophia was crazy.

On their way to see Helena, they didn't speak, not about the coming election or the candidates or the weather, Sophia's clients, Werner's new apprentice, the garden in the back, or the many items on their usual talk list. Nothing. That was unusual. They always had animated conversation about something. She also turned on the radio. Also weird. Sophia didn't like to listen to the radio when she was in the car.

"How come you don't tease me?" Sophia finally said, almost shyly, barely heard above the radio music.

Werner looked over at her and could tell from her expression that she was upset.

He waited too long to answer. Sophia said:

"That's all right. I get it."

The situation was one she had faced her whole life with men. When she was much younger, she would ask: What's wrong with me? No one flirts with me. No one seems to want me. Why is he asking out her and not me? They're not better looking, they're not more interesting, they don't have better personalities? Why? 'Do I give off signals or something?' she thought. 'Have I always given off signals?'

"You're not like other women," Werner finally explained.

"I'm not?"

Werner shook his head.

Tears now were very close for Sophia. That issue was heartbreaking for her. And that was not the answer she was hoping to hear.

"So who's going to win the World Series?" Sophia said loudly, to blast away that train of thought.

Before Werner could reply, she turned up the radio more loudly.

Another long series of empty moments as they passed one street after another, the rain still coming down hard.

Finally, they arrived. Sophia opened the door, but Werner reached over and held her arm.

"I think it's time."

"What do you mean?" Sophia asked.

"We should have coffee."

She stared into his eyes and a smile came on his lips.

"You think so?" she asked.

"Don't you?"

"Suppose it's uncomfortable?" Sophia spoke what she only thought.

"Do you want to say no?"

"I don't know," she replied.

He let go of her arm, leaned over and kissed her cheek.

She got out of the car and walked up to the house, then hurried back.

"Will you become a liberal?"

"I doubt it, not with their record."

She entered the house and returned in a half-hour.

They drove home.

Another long period in which there were no words. Both looked straight ahead.

"I'm not going to become a conservative, Werner. I'm not going to change. I'm too old."

"I know that. We're who we are, gal. That's OK."

"OK," she said, "let's go for coffee."

"And then the porch?" Werner asked.

She looked over at him and it was her turn to smile.

THE END

Under the Smelly Crust

A gentle whistle blew. The massive white iron doors began to shut. The group could hear the end of sound, as each car horn, whirr of the wind, bird song, human voices, and aural signs of existence one by one began slowly to disappear. Finally, the grand door, as high as the ceiling, slammed shut and left a silence marking the end of din against the spirit.

They had no knowledge of how they arrived. They were not asleep or in a dream. No one there was familiar to them. The occasion was not social. There was no feeling of time. Though others were present, each was alone. They did have the sense that this was special, whatever "this" was, and doubted it would happen again.

After the door closed, the great shades on the windows flowed upward and let in a light that was unlike any light they had ever known, a chunky and sweet light ready to be tasted, a restful, warm and uplifting light. The light revealed a soft ceiling of blue that did not seem flat or solid, but as something they could put their hand through; a ceiling in which the stars would want to belong. There followed a quiet hiss and an incense that evoked a soothing feeling of peace, slowed the race of their thoughts down, and somewhat hid the disturbing odor to come.

Beyond the windows and ceiling there were no distinguishing traits, paintings or sculptures, or any sign of a particular age or culture. The space seemed full of potential and yet there was nothing specific to explain why it had that feeling. As an environment, it was quite plain, nothing to distract or enthrall, a scrumptious nothingness.

Each reacted to the combination of the light, ceiling, and smell differently, or identified it as something different, but the effect on them was the same. A crust of stress and anxiety cracked within each of them and a shell fell away, leaving the stink of a life near death, like the smell of flesh after a cast is removed. They stepped outside that cocoon and were lighter versions of themselves. No one complained or felt that they wanted that crust back. They willingly let it go, even though it had become part of them and their way of living. The odor and effect were jarring at first and the lighter version made each of them dizzy, but it also unleashed a creative power deep within them, the power of their identity, their being, and a surge of new life.

No one could instruct them in using that power. It was in them, no doubt about that, but it was long buried by their own burying activities. After years of letting it lay there deep inside but shrouded, its powers entombed under the smelly crust, they were able to see the light of its truth and its possibilities.

At first the participants began to scour through their conscious thoughts and memories not only to comprehend what they were experiencing without the crust, but what they had endured in their existence to that point. Step by step they were seeing how they lived and the choices they had made as they piled the stench and muck of existence upon the art within them. In their present lighter selves without the crust this vision was uncomfortable to undergo for each of them. Why, they asked, had they made these choices that engendered the burying? Continually the light that wanted to spew forth from the inner art was obscured by the heavy needs and desires of existence. The burying incentive was strong because they more and more believed in the needs of existence and no longer felt or believed in the potent light of the art. They noticed that the burying acts were not simply moral or ethical choices; they were choices dominated by the needs of existence. Though the inner art did not demean existence, it did not concern existence and its selfish and superficial tendencies. The art had a different target, something that had no name, but was subtle, with depth, empathy and compassion.

This seemingly endless habit of feeding the needs of existence and loading those needs upon their being, they could plainly see, was both warping their identity and, not surprisingly, was shaping the kind of society in which they now existed.

Observing themselves construct a false and rotting existence was an important step in the process, but it was insufficient alone. Now seeing the effects of their choices with their crusts off, how these products of existence had become false, were deadly, and had affected the life in them, they were given the opportunity to unleash the art within them. That art wanted to transcend the making of death. But to take this step, they had to know how they had practiced death in suffocating their inner art of life and identity. They had to recognize the falseness of the lives and the passion for the dead stuff of the artificial. So the long process of learning how they practiced death ensued. This activity, now unhampered by the crust, came from a deep creative art to make a different being.

In time the exposure in the great hall would end. The massive white door opened, the shades came down, and the participants departed, their crusts once more having returned, and the experience gone from their consciousness. They had all been given this one opportunity to recall and learn their own art of being, and their inner mind, their spirit, would remember and would have that resource to be hopefully used to melt away what had stifled them. The experience in the great hall had shown them how to remove the products of death and desire by practicing and letting the art in each of them shine forth.

THE END

Unwrapped

Talia and a large group were crowded outside the doctor's office. One of the group held a Christmas present.

Talia was pleading with the doctor, but the doctor continued to shake his head as she spoke.

"But he needs to see us!" Talia said in an anxious tone. "How can anything change if he never sees us?"

"Barlow doesn't even know himself," the doctor calmly replied, "let alone you. His mind has blocked his identity, his history, and his view of the world. You must be patient. He has witnessed horrors we can only imagine."

"But it's Christmas," she reminded him. "Again. This is his third Christmas in here. I need to see him. We need to see him. He needs to know we exist. You said this might be the year."

"I'm sorry, I was hoping it might be. But it's not a good idea. If things change, I will immediately contact you."

"But doctor…"

"Let him have his peace, Talia. Let his mind restore itself. It takes time."

"OK fine," she said. "Here, please give him this," handing the doctor a beautiful wrapped box, with sparkling red wrapping paper, with a giant silver bow tied around it.

"Talia," the doctor said, his tone becoming more impatient, "you know he will ignore it. We have a whole closet of gifts from you and his family, all unwrapped, all unopened. One day—"

"Just try, please. Set it down in front of him."

The doctor, frustrated from Talia's constant harassment over the last three years, as well as the repetition of this scene every Christmas, reluctantly nodded and accepted the gift.

"Can we at least watch how he reacts?" Talia asked.

"Come with me," the doctor said. "You can view him from outside the door window."

The door "window" was barely a window, even less a place to view. The main window for observing the room was in the attendant's office next to the entrance, but no one could enter without a security pass.

Talia and her group one by one peeked through the small oval shaped piece of glass in the door at a large room with several sets of tables and chairs. Around the periphery were well-worn couches and chairs. The walls, the chairs, the couches and the ceiling had a light tan color, the patients wore the same pajama-type clothes in a common brownish hue. There was nothing hung on the walls, tables were empty of objects except for a few paperback books and cloth versions of a few board games. There were no windows. Two televisions were on at opposite ends of the room, each tuned to a different channel, both behind protective wire.

The attendant placed on the table before Barlow the bright and glistening gift. Barlow, a young man of twenty-eight, with black hair cut close to his head, sitting alone, slouching on his elbows, his eyes red, his face still wet from the constant barrage of conflict in his mind, ignored the gift. But to the other patients in the room, it was as if a bolt of light had shot into the room, a gong that woke them up and immediately sparked their interest. Slowly and hesitantly—they expected to be ushered away by an attendant—they gathered around Barlow's table and stared at it. Some of them dared to reach over and softly pet the gift. A few said, "Ooh," nodding their heads to show their delight.

The attendant gestured that they should move away, but they still remained close enough to feel part of the event.

"A gift for you, Barlow," the attendant said. "Go ahead. Open it."

Talia lifted up the children so they could see.

"That's Uncle Barlow?" one of them said.

She nodded.

When Talia saw Barlow, even through the tiny window, his face ignited so many good memories, many of them happening in the single year of their marriage. After one year, he was gone, shipped overseas. A few months later he returned, mentally paralyzed by the experience, unwilling to talk about it, unable to function, needing urgent care, in great mental pain.

"He wears the necklace?" Talia quietly said to the doctor. "You let him have it?"

"Oh, we have had a time with that," the doctor explained. "Every day we had to fight with him. The attendants worried he could strangle himself. But he treasured it so much. So now we remove it when he's alone and then give it to him in the lounge. You should see him each day when he enters the lounge. Like a little kid being given his toy."

The attendant waited a few minutes then picked up the present.

"Leave the gift for a while," the doctor instructed. "Keep an eye that none of the others come near it."

Talia was looking around the room and noticed again, like in every year, an important element was missing.

"Again, no sign of Christmas," Talia said. "Couldn't Christmas be a catalyst, doctor, a bell that might ring in someone's head? It could be healing. Barlow has many Christmas memories."

"I'm sorry, Talia, but we can't take a chance with the ornaments, wires, lights, or anything attached to the tree, walls or ceiling. These men are not well. They could use it to hurt themselves or the attendants."

"What about Christmas music?"

"Most of these patients can't distinguish one day from another."

"So, when do you think it will happen?" Talia said. "Will there be no chance for us to sit in a visiting room with him, even if doesn't know us."

"Talia, please understand and trust me. Such an experience would be overwhelming for Barlow. You see him? He's in a sealed shell. Some of the other men will mingle, play games, or chat. Not Barlow. He's not there yet. He's numb, hurting. His time will come, but not now."

"Fine. But I'm worried that you might forget who he is. You've never seen the real man. That shell is not him. Don't give up on him, Doc. He's special, a good man. He has helped many others. Now he needs help. You'll see when he's back to being himself. Do you know what he once did? In freezing weather, brutal snow storm, he went out to free a rat that was pinned by an old fence. That's my man, OK? Kids love him. In the fighting, he was brave...and he's so kind...he..."

Talia was faltering from her thoughts of him before he went overseas.

"I know, I know," the doctor said gently. "You've told me. We're taking good care of him. But there's no time table for how the mind heals."

Talia would have remained forever at the small piece of glass, if they would have let her. Near Barlow was her only place of peace. She had asked the doctor in the first year if she could rent a room that wasn't used so that, when she wasn't working, she could be near him. The doctor said that was not possible. It would be unfair to the many others who feel the same way as she.

"Ask the attendant to open it," Talia blurted out.

"What?" the doctor asked. She had never before requested the present be unwrapped by someone else.

"Yes, please ask the attendant to unwrap the present."

As the attendant took off the neatly tied flamboyant silver bow and then tediously removed the wrapping, the other patients came as close as possible to the table to see what was inside.

Meanwhile, Barlow had not changed his demeanor, except to put his head in his hands and look down so that no one could see his face.

The attendant set the wrapping aside and opened the box. It was an album filled with photos of his life.

"Turn the pages slowly," Talia instructed, "so Barlow has time to see the photographs."

The attendant did as she said. Some of the patients were quite excited, but Barlow remained motionless. Twenty pages of the album had passed before Barlow brought his head up and looked at the album. The attendant had already passed by his baby pictures, him on his bicycle, in his first suit, his first dog Whipper sitting waiting for a treat, the year he broke his elbow and had a cast, a picture of his father and him out shoveling during a snow storm, another at the beach when his family rented a cottage, many pictures of Christmas dinners, opening presents in his pajamas, another when he was standing in front of his school in his graduation gown, he with his three best friends Jed, Peter and Udan at the bachelor party, and many others; but then, near the last ten pages, there were photographs of when Talia entered his life, first a photograph her friend took of her looking at him before they dated—though he always said he loved her long before she knew he existed—and the years of dating before the wedding, a photo of her dragging him to hockey games, and him dragging her to baseball games, the Christmas market in their Santa hats, a photo of the old car in which they would have their long chats outside her house, the honeymoon in Mexico with each in sombreros, a photo of her hugging him in uniform, and many others; but as the attendant was about to turn the last page, Barlow's hand came out of nowhere and placed it on a page on which was a poorly focused photo he took of her at Pizza Hut when he gave her the necklace because he couldn't yet afford the right ring; and in the photo Talia beamed with such happiness that her eyes were starting to water up. Barlow stared at the photograph a long time and then, with his other hand, grabbed the necklace around his neck.

Behind the door and the tiny window, Talia was so overwhelmed she slid to the floor, closed her eyes, and began slowly to cry. It wasn't the happiest day of her life—that was when she married Barlow—but it came very close.

THE END

FLASH FICTION
(stories under 1000 words)

Before Father Lost his Mind

Before father lost his mind, we talked of his estate, and he said, "Come every month on the days when it rains, recite King Lear, and it's yours."

Now we stand beside his lawyer outside his open window on rainy days and repeatedly recite King Lear from start to finish while our father with dementia listens but does not recognize us. When we reach Act I, Scene 4, he puts his head out the window and screams Lear's line with us, "How sharper than a serpent's tooth it is to have a thankless child!" and then returns to silence.

The End

BILL DIED AND LEFT ME A PIG

Bill died and left me a pig I swear is Bill.

My wife Ellen smirks, "Really? Bill is Hardy the pig?"

When that pig approaches me, he shakes his bottom, smiles, his tongue hangs then stiffens. Hardy always winks at me with strange eyes, too red for a pig, then turns and farts.

In private I scold it, even whip it for mocking me.

"You need help," Ellen says and makes an appointment.

The doctors ignore me.

The priest holds my hand and prays.

Only the fish in the waiting room agrees.

"You're right," it says, "Hardy loves your wife."

The End

THE BRAND OF A

It's tough to recall my days and nights of wild delights when blood was smearing sidewalks. It's painful to remember how I turned aside my eyes, shut my ears, and ignored the daily power shortages. It's hard to forget when I set aside the daily news and stayed at home and watching while others marched, retook the streets, and fought for change and liberty.

They saw me through my window as I read and watched them from my sitting room. And when the revolution ended, they dragged me to the street in front of neighbors, burned the letter A into my flesh, and jailed me in my house—now painted red for all to see.

The scar was deep. I felt it every day and hid it with a scarf, though I had to show it to anyone who asked. Even children wanted to boast to friends they'd seen it.

I had no friends. I worked with the other branded ones, but we weren't allowed to socialize outside work.

Yearly they herded us to the public squares to show us and give a speech.

"Here!" they proclaimed. "Look at the ones who didn't care. Look at their brand! Observe the brand of A! Remember where they lived and how they stood and watched! And know this: if we all had been like they were, we would now live in tyranny and with no freedom. Don't feel sorry for them. It's the only end for these creatures of apathy."

When the old regime returned to power, the reverse occurred. Now those marked with the letter A were decorated and the new leaders showcased us as heroes.

As I rode down the street in holiday parades, the same people who once jeered and avoided me now shouted and waved.

I do not blame them or feel bitter. I was neutral during the revolution and I was neutral during the return of the old regime. Who knows if the revolution returns again?

If only that letter A could mean activist and not apathy.

THE END

THE CLEANING OF ST. MATTHEWS

St. Matthews yesterday closed. The organ played. The old people gathered, sang and prayed. They mourned the end of worship, then used the toilet.

I scrubbed everything clean.

Next the racoons, rats, bears, and animals without fear of vacant sacred places roamed and made their marks. Birds flocked to the steeple and pooped everywhere.

No worries for a caretaker. I will clean up their mess. I'm always here. The graveyard duties alone keep me busy. All will stay spotless until the next crisis and the people return. The organ will play again. There will be much praying and singing. Afterwards, they will use the toilet. As long as there's a mess, St Matthews and I are happy.

The End

The Weather Died

As the minority warned, the birds did not return. Spring failed to come. Lake Lynx did not melt. Only drifts and icicles buttressed by a cold, unwavering wind remained.

In panic residents full of alcohol gathered and believed winter would pass.

"No it won't!" the minority screamed and so frightened the residents that they jailed the dissenters.

Only time passed. The weather died from lack of change.

"Why are you surprised?" the minority bravely shouted behind the bars.

The people moved away, leaving their town encased in frost, their land entombed in snow, and their prophets forgotten in jail.

The End

Lawn or Car

Whenever Taylor's neighbor George massages his new car, white mounds of soap flow over and destroy the edges of Taylor's lawn.

This angers Taylor, especially when George ignores his own lawn and lets weeds and dandelions flourish.

"You're killing my lawn," Taylor tells George.

"You're embarrassing the neighborhood with that piece of junk," George replied, pointing at Taylor's old and rusty car. "When you gonna get rid of it?"

"What?"

"The broken-down Fiat. It's ugly and it's dangerous. Your wife must worry when she drives it."

"When you gonna clean up your lawn so it isn't an eyesore in the neighborhood?" Taylor replies.

That comment stops the conversation for a quarter of an hour.

"Tell you what," George finally says. "I'll take care of the lawn, you buy a new car."

Taylor gladly agrees. He buys a new Fiat and George removes the old lawn and starts fresh.

George finds his new lawn quite attractive, but now worries that the weeds will return. So he puts his car into the garage and sprays his lawn with toxic pesticide each week. The dust not only blows upon Taylor's lawn but into his lungs and throughout the entire neighborhood.

For inexplicable reasons, despite George's spraying, Taylor now has a serious weed problem. Taylor spends each evening after work weeding.

"Your weeds are now spreading to my lawn," George informs Taylor.

Taylor looks at him with scornful eyes.

He's now telling me how to handle my lawn!

Taylor calls the city and reports the pesticides, explaining that George's lawn is too near the school. The school children walk by each day and the cancerous dust is covering the schoolyards.

The city visits George and warns him that his spraying is a hazard. He must stop.

The news deflates George's enthusiasm. He lets his lawn decline. The weeds once again return. Strangely Taylor's lawn has fewer and fewer weeds.

George now compliments Taylor's lawn and Taylor speaks highly of George's car.

THE END

JERROLD'S AGREEMENT

Jerrold left for Syria seeking the terrorists who held him hostage.

Before the abduction Jerrold was a stockbroker who led a life of excessive indulgence and extravagance. On business in Istanbul, partying with his chums at a private club, the terrorists came as masked men and abducted him and others. They tried to ransom him, but his company was silent, his family and he had insufficient funds, and his government would not negotiate.

Silvia, one of the Istanbul club dancers, was in the cell beside him. They became friends and supported each other through the ordeal.

The abductors released him but kept her, a daughter from a wealthy family.

Jerrold promised to come back and rescue her, but the abductors laughed.

"Don't count on it, woman! That's a snake who only cares about himself."

*

Surprised to see Jerrold return as promised, Spider, the leader, asked why.

"To save Silvia. If I had never met Silvia, I would be living a different life. She's a friend and gave me strength."

Spider could not believe he was hearing these ironic words.

"You came back for Silvia. How sweet! But do you have the money?"

"No."

"Why then should I release her?"

"A contest."

"Hand-to-hand combat?"

"No, I'm not a warrior," Jerrold said. "Instead, test me, test my worth. If I meet your standards, release her."

"You? You the partier, the addict, the guy without a faith, and a hundred girlfriends? You symbolize what we despise. You fight for money and corruption and let your women walk around half undressed. Go home before I change my mind. You're worth nothing to anyone. No one would ransom you and you haven't the character to win back another. Silvia stays until her family pays the ransom."

"You're afraid I might succeed," Jerrold taunted.

"No, I'm not," Spider said. "You're so typical of the weak Westerner with bad habits. You say you've changed, but you'll return to your habits."

"Some of your people are Westerners," Jerrold said.

"None of them was ever like you. Weak in body, weaker in mind, weakest in morals and ethics, that's why your kind will lose. Our age will not degenerate like yours."

"You've known too few of us," Jerrold said.

"Your past behavior doomed you. Habits, not words or money, impress."

"Can I see her?" Jerrold asked.

Her captors brought Silvia out, stumbling, barely able to walk, her eyes closed, her head wobbly, her face and clothes dirty, screaming how she wanted to stay.

Spider shrugged and laughed.

"I'm afraid she wants to stay. Go home, and join your decadent West in its final years."

Spider gestured to one of his soldiers.

"Take him away and kill him if he returns."

As the soldier grabbed Jerrold, Silvia snatched a hand automatic from an unsuspecting guard and pressed it up to Spider's head.

"Give him a chance or I'll pull the trigger," she screamed. "You know I will! I don't care! I've had it with you!"

"Fine," Spider said with a smirk.

"Say: 'I promise before God the Almighty.' Now!"

Spider wiped away his smile and hesitated.

"I promise before God the Almighty," Spider said. "God is merciful."

Silvia threw the gun to the ground and returned to her tent.

Spider then grabbed Jerrold's arm and brought him to a place outside the ears of others.

"You have your chance," he said. "I'm bound by my word before God and my people. Go home. We'll watch your behavior for six months. If you lead a moral life, Silvia will be free.

"However," Spider continued, his face almost touching Jerrold's face, "since I was forced into this agreement, there's more. Even if you behave for six months and free Silvia, that won't be enough. We'll continue to check on you as long as you live. If you return to your old dissolute life, we will know, and the consequences will be severe, not only for you, but for all of the residents of your city. This too I promise before almighty God. The lives of many depend upon the quality of your life."

*

Till he was an old man Jerrold looked at his city in a way quite different from anyone else. Some days he wanted to die to free himself from Spider's awful threat because he worried his acts might not meet the standard of Spider or those who watched him. There was a chance that Spider was dead and no one remembered him. But he would not take the chance. Every time he read a newspaper about a terrorist threat or suicide bomber he shuddered to think of the burden and responsibility Spider had thrust upon him. Even if he wondered at times if anyone was truly watching him, he never doubted Spider would fulfill his threat. Jerrold would not sacrifice the entire population of his city because he did not live a life of quality.

On his eightieth birthday, he took a walk to a park and sat upon a bench. He was there for only a few minutes when another old man sat down beside him.

"I didn't think you could do it, Jerrold," the man said. "You're free."

THE END

Screams

Josh tried to open the front door of his house without success. Finally he smashed it down and found the rooms empty except for trash, uneaten food, rats, and scraps of wood. His wife and child did not come to meet him.

He walked back out and in tears he wondered: *This is my home, but the place is falling down and rotting.* He said out loud on the front steps: "Where's my life? Where's my family?"

The tree in the front yard was full of pink blossoms that would create a gorgeous space of color on the lawn. *That memory at least had not passed.* Nor had his wish to pick the blossoms, but as he did, a scream burst from the house.

He ran through the door and the screaming stopped.

Sounds came from the upstairs. He slowly climbed the stairs until he stood in front of his child's bedroom. The door, broken on its hinges, creaked open and Josh faced a large creature sitting in the middle of the floor eating pieces of wood from a child's chair.

"This house tastes good," the creature said. "It has sweetness and joy. I love it."

"You've eaten everything?" Josh asked.

"Yes, just about done. I'm going to leave the cellar till the end. It smells so delicious. It'll be my dessert. I treasure cellars and attics. Oh, the attic, I must say, was a yummy delight, not at all the usual dusty garbage."

"Where's my family?"

"Your what? There's only furniture, chairs, desks, beds, picture frames and cribs. Oh, did I relish the rocking chair."

"I lived here with my wife and child."

"Sorry, I know nothing about that."

"I heard a scream. There must be people."

"Oh the scream! Why didn't you say? Yes, screams happen. People don't want me to eat the house. And this house. Well, over the years, lots of people lived here. You know, their memories, stuff like that. The place meant a lot to them. Even the tragedies. So they scream."

Josh left the creature and went downstairs to where the living room was. He then released a scream that in length and volume added up to eighty years of wonderful life.

Waving Goodbye

The minister, waist deep in the water, was reading some words from scripture and Talia and Ethan were waiting for their turn to walk down into the font. Every pew in the church was full and every person in the pews, Ethan felt, was staring at him and Talia.

Each wore a long white thread-bare robe, the same robes that many other adolescents had worn at every baptism.

Talia, pressed up against him, looked at Ethan with a nervous smile. He smiled back.

He tried to pretend that he was unconcerned and not thinking about what his friends and he had talked about at school. But the conflict between that conversation and what he should be thinking was making him uncomfortable. This was a sacred event. It was not a time to think about whether he would see clearly, clearer than anyone should, how her body looked once her robe became wet and stuck to her skin.

The closeness of Talia's body beside him did not help. She reached over and took his hand and grabbed it tightly, placing it against her thigh. She was quivering.

The minister then called her name and she walked down into the water. Ethan watched her form disappear as the minister leaned her backwards and baptized her.

Don't look, Ethan said to himself, *look somewhere else.*

"Now put on the Lord Jesus Christ and make no provision for the flesh…," the minister quoted scripture.

As she emerged from the water and walked up the steps his eyes seemed out of his control and focused on her naked form visible under the clinging wet garment.

The minister noticed his gawking and scowled at him. The congregation could see that his face had turned red, but Ethan's mother later explained he was nervous and worried about the event.

Ethan next heard his name and walked down into the font. The water was cold, smelled of chorine, and felt thick.

"Blessed Assurance," came from the organ.

As he looked up at the rafters of the church, he swore he could see his own form smiling and waving. He closed his eyes and looked again. His form remained.

Ethan discreetly pointed up at it to show the minister.

The minister ignored him and continued to speak the ceremonial words. Then he asked Ethan if he was willing to accept Jesus Christ and follow his principles.

Ethan said yes and the minister submerged Ethan's body. Under the water the vision on the ceiling remained, but it disappeared when the minister brought him out.

Shivering from the water, Ethan quickly walked back up the steps on the other side of the font and joined Talia and the minister's wife out of sight of the congregation.

Talia was now wrapped up with a couple of towels standing next to the minister's wife, both ogling at his own wet nakedness beneath the robe that glued to his flesh regardless how he tried to pull it away. He covered himself with his hands.

Talia handed him a towel and said happily, "We did it. We're reborn."

"Yes, we're reborn," he said less enthusiastically.

One side of him was excited to believe in the ritual and vision, while the other was unable to erase the image of the soaked garment painting Talia's shape, leaving only a thin fabric between her glistening skin and the ways of eternity.

THE END

DON'T STOP

You try to have high standards, praise wisdom and knowledge, strive to make yourself moral and ethical. You sit reading *Nightwood* while listening to the music of Laurie Anderson and glance occasionally at a copy of Bridgit Riley's "Shadow Play" on the wall of your living room. Each week you attend your faith and volunteer at the homeless shelter or food drive. It's a quiet, simple, harmless, and unthreatening life, without changes.

From James in the apartment next door comes the smell of alcohol and marijuana, the noise of activists out to change the world, and the laughter of his newest lover. You fall asleep to the noise of their pleasure and enthusiasm.

James one day sees you in the elevator carrying a book.

"What you reading there?"

"*Behind the Beautiful Forevers* by Katherine Boo," you say.

"What a life you have!" James says. "To revel in art, ideas, and music, to live quietly and meditate, help the homeless and hungry. I say to my friends, 'That neighbor of mine next door, now there's a hero.'"

You think but do not say: 'What? I'm a hero? I do nothing. What have I ever done?'

"Whereas look at me," James complains, "what do I accomplish? I talk, march, drink, smoke, and put up posters. I protest, but nothing happens. Nothing changes. God, what a loser!"

His face is sad and frustrated, waiting for your reaction.

We exit the elevator.

You grab his arm gently.

"Don't stop what you do," you say. "We need you."

"You too," he answers.

The End

Wood

The clock on the kitchen wall was wooden. So were the kitchen table and the cupboards and the holders for the knives and the chairs. They were all wooden. Wood! I hate it! I hate wood. Bring me the documents, but paper, no paper. Beverly, get in here and shut the door. There's no guardian, you know. You can't imagine Phillipa sitting there with that spoon, can you? Can you? The clock did not work. It was wood. It was just a display for the elves. The thing floats, right? Scotland, honey, next year. We're get one of those cuckoo clocks, right? The wood of the table started to drip brown drip. All over the floor. Sit down, have a pint. Look at you, only twenty years old, so sweet. I once saw a man in the park singing love songs to some ducks in the pond. The ducks on the clock sat on the table and spewed out water until Phillipa threw spoons at the cat and fell against the door and the ducks were wooden replicas. All year long I watched the people on the screen say, Oh Say Can You See, and there was wood on the arms of the chair, right at the end, and I was laughing when Phillipa cried because of that show Woody H was in, or was it that Woody in Toy Story or what did she call the thing, something about—no, it was Woody A—and I saw them in the woods somewhere, down by the pond with ducks or swan and some boy threw a branch and hit the boat two lovers were in—oh no that was Central Park in 2012 when when...tell the story, tell the story...Shakespeare, oh how the woodcock strives for the gin, yeah, Henry, oh I hide in the woods and wait to spy on Phillipa in the boat with Woodford, big Dick Woodford, and that was where? Oh Say Can You See. Has he eaten? Give him a wooden spoon, he likes wood. Give him a wooden bowl too. He'll eat anything in a wooden bowl. Look at the bowl melting, Beverly. Gooey. Messy. Close it up, he's dead. I'm not. I'm not. That's a fine coffin. What kind of wood is that? In 200 days Uncle Fred's coming with his boat and that bat he promised you. I want you to play ball with him. Go off in the woods to the field and hit some balls, ok? You'll love his bat. It has no knots. None. Phillipa, please help me. I can hear you. I'm in the Rosewood Buddha statue watching her do yoga. "The parmesan cheese you sprinkle on the penne could be sawdust." Hahaha. Serves the little people flying around who eat my pasta. I see them. I see Barney and Stick and Root and the television cabinet that Uncle Fred used. They have wooden cereal boxes in here and the breakfast tastes like wood chips. Wood chips! I don't want it! Eat your own sawdust, Beverly! Ooh! she moaned. I would like see all the wood in the room stand up, wouldn't you Beverly. Hahaha. Sawdust in the basement. In the year 2001, three villages were hungry for lack of wood, so they got down on their knees and looked up to the sky and asked the wood god for food, and the wood god said, Look to the roof, I will be there, I will pour down fir and oak and maple and banana and beech and birch and bitch and baby and stop it! Stop it! You're hurting me. The Professor said: The forests are disappearing, the forests are disappearing. I saw my dead wife yesterday eating at the ceiling with a little elf and the elf said, Get out while you can, this wood is rotten, can't you smell it, Henry? I can. That's why I'm with the elves. Every day they come at 2 pm and the room is full of them. Look! There! They say, Cook it with cream. There's no Totem Poles anymore. The Totem Poles are disappearing. We got that little one from a shop at Mount Rushmore. Beverly, come here. Show me. Show me more. Give me those documents. When's the appointment? We have lots of carvings of ducks and birds. I want one, Mom. I see you, honey, I'll be up there singing with the elves your songs, so easy to love. 2 pm. 2 pm. 2 pm. You wanna play dominoes. They're nice big wooden ones so you see the dots. I think a wild wonderful wacky woeful winsome woody wedding is just fine, but invite Beverly, ok Phillipa, ok please? Whoa boy. Calm down. You'll see her again. Wood burns. Fire kills. Everything's made of wood. Phillipa, forgive the wood god. He hates summer too.

THE END

The Art of Flying

When Filmore turned thirteen, she took the test and flew. Filmore had no wings, experience, or knowledge of flying. She thought: Take the mandatory test and return home to Mom and Dad. When the examiners watched her fly, immediately they caged her so she could not fly away, and rushed her to the place for girls who fly. Her parents and girlfriends looked on helplessly and cried. In a few years they brought her home, an older and changed person. When the next mandatory test came, she knew how to fail. She also knew when to fly.

THE END

Closing the Window on a Hot Summer Night

Twelve-year old Thessy sat behind her father Ethan as he drove her home from ballet practice. There were several ways to reach home, but Ethan took the quickest. For Thessy it was the scariest. His route went through the old industrial district which had very few street lights and was like entering a ghost town even in the day time. At night it had an eerie feeling as if danger was nearby and zombies could rush at her from any direction.

Thessy looked out her open window, her mouth open, staring into the large dark empty parking lots and buildings with graffiti and havens for the homeless and drug addicts. Occasionally she would hear the distant sound of voices or see a flicker from a cigarette lighter or match through the veil of darkness and then a shadow pass quickly before it. It was a hot summer night, but she kept her finger on the window button, prepared to shut it if anyone came near. As her heart beat quickened, she kept repeating in her mind, 'hurry, Daddy, hurry.'

The need to hurry was especially nerve-wracking about half way through the stretch when the road curved in an S and any driver would need to reduce speed. In that area, the car slowed to such an extent, she would grip the front seat in fear and imagine a person could jump into their car or pull out people in the car.

As they neared the section, she noticed a group of people behind several large garbage receptacles.

"Daddy, there's some people up ahead. Hurry."

As they passed the receptacles, a woman jumped out from behind one of them and was running toward their car. She was in her panties and bra and had bloody scratches and marks on her arms and chest.

"Help me!" she screamed desperately. "Let me get in. Please!"

"Close the window, Thessy, quick!" her father yelled.

Thessy did as she was told. The automatic window started to close, but an arm of the woman was caught in it. Thessy opened it so she could free the arm, and then Thessy and her father sped off.

"No, no, please come back! Please!" the woman shouted as she continued to run after their car.

Thessy looked at her through the rear window. Three men appeared, grabbed her and dragged her to a place behind the receptacles.

"Don't tell your mother about this," her father said when he looked at his shaking daughter in the rear-view mirror. "She worries enough about you. In fact, it's best not to tell anyone about what happened."

Thessy, still looking through the rear window, nodded and began to cry.

"You understand, sweetie. I couldn't take the chance. They might have taken you."

In a few days the police found in one of the receptacles the body of a young woman abducted from a party only three streets away from Thessy's home.

Her father never took that route again on ballet night, but often, when Thessy looked at herself in the rear-view mirror or at her father, she would relive that event, especially the arm caught in the window, the woman running after their car, and think about a secret she wished she did not have.

The End

Dogs and Insects

"I haven't got it just one more week you'll see" *but I know I'll never get it and feel little slivers under the skin erupt* "I don't have the money" "get it somewhere you can come back find someplace else get a tent camp on the beach people sometimes drop wallets or money wait till dark and the beach clears" *the lake is so quiet little waves slap the shore a couple down the way kissing only the light of the moon now the couple leaves I'm alone without a tent I'll sleep under a picnic table on my bags it's so quiet except for the water I try to imagine I'm home where will I get the money why did I leave home what was that I heard something* "where'd you last see him" "right here or near here I remember the swings and that drinking fountain" "OK don't cry call him" "SNOWBALL" "we'll find him he's all white *I know that dog I saw that dog* "it's scary here at night daddy let's go back to the campsite" "I thought you wanted to find your dog" "it's too dark Daddy" *I lay on my back looking at the moldy underside of the picnic table and the home of unwanted insects and I wonder how many hours till dawn feeling so alone what am I going to do should I go home they'll be upset and say I told you so but I can't stay I have no friends no job or place to live what's that a rain drop oh no come on no rain but it rains I hear a dog bark and then its face looks at me under the table barks again and comes beside me to avoid the rain its big black nose sniffing my cheek it lays down is it Snowball no this is a brown dog then I hear footsteps* "what you doing under there sweetie want company" *but the dog growls viciously at the man* "that's my dog let me have him" *I say nothing the dog snaps at the man when he tries to grab it* "push the dog out" *I do nothing* "you better come you mutt or I'm going to beat you" *the man leaves and returns with a thick stick and tries to strike one time he hits the dog hard but the dog growls and fights back and bites the man and the man leaves but the dog is hurt and whimpers I pet it try to speak gently to the dog until day break when we crawl out from under the table and walk together the dog limping and I longing for home*

THE END

THE END of COLLECTION